Introduction

It was dark and it must have been around 11 p.m. at night, early in the year during the winter months. The roads were empty. I was driving on a long, winding country road, on my way home from work.

I had been working late a lot. I was about 23, and the world was in the middle of the 2008/9 recession. I was tired and stressed, and I felt like I was going nowhere. I had felt that way for quite some time because no matter how hard I tried or how hard I worked, no matter how patient I was and how hard I tried to stay positive, it felt like nothing was breaking my way. I had been struggling for a few years at that point, trying to find my way in the world.

But I was exhausted. I had been trying so hard for so long; it just felt like it was never going to happen for me. I was depressed and lonely, but above all, I was angry. I was frustrated with the lack of progress in my life. I was far behind the expectations I had put on myself, I wasn't happy, and I hated myself. I had failed to achieve my potential; I was a worthless nobody, and I didn't deserve to be happy.

As these thoughts raced through my mind, a wave of emotion came flooding over me. The tears began to flow, and my body began to shake. I was scared. I began to envision a future that involved no happiness that was not momentary or fleeting. All I could see was the dark. A cold and lonely future full of frustration, failure, and misery. I felt so much pain in my heart. I was crying hard. I should not have been driving. I felt so alone. I couldn't take any more of the pain that I was feeling. I wanted it to end.

I must have been going at 80 miles an hour. I was over the speed limit and almost willing my car to lose control. I wasn't looking at the road. I was imagining crashing my car into a tree or hitting a ditch and rolling in a ball of flames. I was willing myself to do it. Tears were streaming down my face. In that moment, I wanted to die.

At least, that's what I thought.

The Truth Behind the Smile

My mental health journey and the lessons I have learnt along the way

SIMON GEORGE

Disclaimer

I am just a man sharing my thoughts, my personal opinions, my feelings, and my experiences, as well as the lessons I have learnt and the mental tools I have developed during my life. All the advice, techniques, approaches, and strategies found within this book may not be suitable for everybody and every situation. This work is sold with the understanding that neither the author nor publisher can be held responsible for anything resulting from the advice in this book.

Re-Introduction

Allow me to re-introduce myself. My name is Simon. I am a 34-year-old man from Warwickshire, England. I am single. I am temporarily back living with my parents because I am currently unemployed and have been for the whole of 2020. But I am feeling content within myself and am feeling confident and positive about my future.

I grew up in a village in the countryside. I had a nice and happy childhood. It wasn't until my late teens that things started to unravel. I remember something a friend said to me once in high school. She said that I always smiling. I remember laughing in response but feeling a little confused by the comment. Looking back, there was a time when I believed that was the moment it all changed, but I'm wise enough to know now that this isn't true. Nevertheless, it's a good marker. Because it was not long after this, in my late teens, that I started to struggle with depression and anxiety. A dark mood that would cloud over the next decade of my life was looming, although I didn't know it at the time.

Despite my struggles, I always did my best to make the most of my life. It was a tough uphill struggle, but I did manage to carve out a career in market research (specialising in brands and consumer relationships), which gave me some stability. But there were a lot of challenges and setbacks along the way. What I am most proud of is that no matter how hard I found life, I still managed to pursue my dreams to travel the world (or at least a small portion of it anyway). I ticked off many items from my bucket list, and I immersed myself in this beautiful world that we live in.

I have spent the last two years of my life living in Barcelona, the most recent year of which did not go to plan. I am sure many people can say the same, but I found that my previous years had prepared me to adapt to all the challenges that life throws at me, even during the Covid pandemic. I found myself unemployed and struggling to find work, but I didn't let that break me. I decided to make the most of my time in Barcelona. I maxed out my savings trying to find a way to remain there and to continue my dream. I didn't care about the money—it was worth the sacrifice to support my dream of living abroad.

In the end, I had to return home to live with my parents. Thankfully, I am fortunate enough to have parents who were able to take me in. But despite my plans falling through, despite having to give up on my dream a little earlier than planned, I focused on the positives. I had fulfilled my dream to live abroad. I had made new friends and gained valuable life experiences. It may not have gone to plan, but I tried. I am immensely proud of myself for not letting life dictate how I live. I will continue to take calculated risks for the sake of my happiness. And I will always put my mental health first.

I wrote this book because I believe I have something valuable to share. And by sharing the details from my own mental health journey and the lessons I have learnt, I hope that I can help you with your mental health journey or support a loved one with theirs. If I can help to ease the pain and suffering for you or your loved ones, even just a little, then all of this will have been worth it.

Within this book, you will find the genuine thoughts and feelings I have felt whilst struggling with depression and my mental health in general. I cover a range of areas, not just depression, but also my struggles with anxiety, particularly linked to low self-esteem and self-confidence. I have struggled with both obsessive-compulsive disorder and imposter syndrome (self-diagnosed). I have struggled with loneliness, and, at my lowest, I even battled with suicidal thoughts.

Even though mental health awareness is gaining more momentum these days, we still do not talk about our feelings enough. Especially men. But we all need to learn to be a little more open and trusting with each other. There are many books about mental health, and even more social media blogs. And although some of these are genuinely helpful and inspiring, I find many to be quite cold and clinical or a lot of hot and empty air; promoting positive quotes and empty messages that are instantly lost in our hectic minds or swallowed up by an overload of content. This is why I wanted to write this book; to share an inside perspective of what a real mental health journey looks like.

Everyone's experience with mental health is going to be different and unique to them. But we can often relate to something, and by talking about it more openly, we can help each other to make our own experiences a little easier. Now, I can't promise you solutions, but I do hope that you will learn something valuable from my experiences and the lessons I have learnt along the way.

I am not perfect, but nobody is. I have made many mistakes, but I have tried to learn from them all. I will continue making mistakes and I will continue to learn from them, because that is how we grow as people. I have learnt to fully accept all of who I am, including my flaws. And I am now in a place that allows me to face the challenges of life from a much stronger position than when I started this journey. I no longer let my fears or my worries consume me.

I believe in myself, and you can too.

The Dark Days

It all started when I was about 17/18 years old (back in the early 2000s). I guess that's when you start to become an adult for real and you take control of your life for the first time. I finished high school at 16 and went on to college. I was coming to the end of my college experience, and so it was time for me to choose my path. I needed to choose whether I would be going to university to continue my studies, and which course I wanted to study for the next three or four years. On top of that, I had to decide which university I wanted to go to, whether or not I would be staying on campus, and whether I'd be taking out a loan to pay for my studies. All of a sudden it felt like I had real-life questions to answer for the first time, and I had no answers.

I was young and I had no idea who I was or what I wanted from life, I panicked, I made some wrong choices, and when my plan A collapsed; I was lost with no backup plan and no idea what to do. The dark clouds were forming, and my mind was being taken over by fear and anxiety. I was only 18 years old with my whole future ahead of me and plenty of time to make amends. But at the time, choosing which university and which degree to study felt so overwhelmingly crucial that I was terrified I would make the wrong choice, or I'd fail, and I'd lose out on everything I had ever dreamed of. I put so much pressure on myself that I truly believed that if I did not make the right choice and I did not get my degree, I would never achieve any of my goals.

The fear of failure was just too much. I was young with very little life experience, and I had no clue what career I wanted to pursue. When you're young, you don't realise that you have plenty of time. It's hard to comprehend at the time, but you do not have to have it all figured out. But back in 2004 I still believed that I was meant to get a degree, followed by a successful career, to meet someone and fall in love, get married, have a family, and buy a house—all this before I turned 30. And somewhere in there, I wanted to achieve my dreams too. But why? Who set these rules, these social parameters for living our lives? Who has achieved this perfect life that everyone wants to emulate? Sometimes we let society and other people determine how we should live our own lives, but the truth is, there is no one way to do it.

This may have been before the days of the social media boom, but I still compared myself to others and to my own inflated expectations. I was too critical of myself. I needed to cut myself some slack. Instead, I had put so much pressure on this decision that it was always likely to fail. I felt lost and confused. I had no clear direction, and I had nobody in my life who I felt I could turn to for advice. I felt alone and isolated although I was surrounded by people. I could feel my world beginning to crumble, and I could see the tidal waves of emotion over the horizon. I had no defences; I was unprepared and vulnerable.

The inevitable happened. I made a series of poor choices. I chose a university close to home so I could commute and work at the same time. I wanted to pay my own way through university and avoid debt. I decided not to stay on campus, and I chose a combined course of two subjects with nothing in common (business studies and American studies). I over-compromised; I played it safe and never fully committed to the experience. I was too scared and intimidated to venture off alone and instead, I found myself being pulled in several different directions and never really committing to any of them. I was working a low-skilled job that I did not enjoy (I was a pot washer in a kitchen and had been for several years already), and I judged myself for not having a better one. I was attending a university that I never felt comfortable at, studying a course I no longer saw the point of.

I didn't make any friends, and with my life split between locations I felt like a ghost living two different lives. I was tired and I still felt lost. And most importantly, I was terrified of failure. My anxiety was through the roof and I didn't even know or understand what it was. I was becoming depressed. I would cry myself to sleep at night. I spent every hour of my job hating it and thinking about why I had made such a stupid decision, thinking only negative thoughts about the impact this was having on my life.

At university, I felt lonely and distant. I had no social life; no distractions or relief from the pain I was feeling. My friends were all off living their lives without any idea of what I was going through. In my mind, no one else was struggling; only me. I compared myself to my friends who were all at university making new friends, learning new things, and taking control of their lives. Yet I was in the complete opposite position, becoming more and more obsessed with my imminent failure every day. All I could picture was a sad lonely life with no money, no friends, and no happiness.

It doesn't matter that the reality did not match my thoughts, because I was trapped inside my head. My mental health was in freefall, and neither I nor anybody else even knew that this was a real possibility. I was unintentionally self-sabotaging my life. I needed to reach out to someone, find help, support, and an outlet for my emotions, but instead, it was all being bottled up.

Every day I added new negative thoughts and feelings; I was weighed down by it all. I was tired. I always felt on the verge of tears, and I felt like a failure. I thought it was only me who was suffering, and I couldn't understand why. How could this happen? I was kind, intelligent, and athletic. I paid attention at school and I was a good person. What did I do wrong? What did I do to deserve this? These were real thoughts running through my head every day, and every small little issue would instantly add to the ever-growing burden. It began to feel insurmountable. Moreover, after thinking and feeling all of these things I would suddenly feel guilty. I'd feel guilty and ashamed that I allowed myself to think this way when there were people out there in the world fighting just to stay alive every day. It was a constant rollercoaster ride that I thought would never end, and it was exhausting.

Ultimately, I dropped out of university. But instead of taking time to reflect and process what had happened, I felt the pressure to be doing something productive; anything. I wasn't allowed to be unemployed or to take time out; it just wasn't socially acceptable for me to feel lost. I did not feel that I had the luxury of time to explore different options. I needed to be in full-time work right away—that was the responsible thing to do. So, although I had let go of something that wasn't working and was not positively contributing to my mental health, instead of feeling relief, I went straight into working full-time at the job I hated. My suffering continued. I was being responsible, and I was earning money. But I was unhappy and becoming unhappier every day; the same cycle of thoughts running through my mind day after day after day.

Imagine competing in an endurance assault course; a military-style test that pushes your body and mind to its limits. That's what it felt like I was doing every single day. I was fighting an all-out war in my head. It was a constant battle between my anxiety and my depression to contain and control my negative emotions. I was absolutely drained every day.

This went on for months and months. Even when I had some light relief, like a celebratory occasion with friends or family, a holiday, a funny movie, or a happy song, there was still always a part of me that was conscious of my unhappiness. I always felt that these moments were temporary. I even sometimes felt guilty for feeling happy. I couldn't justify it; I did not deserve it. Nobody in my life had any idea how I felt or what I was going through. Not a single one. And even if they had, I am not sure it would have changed anything. We just had no comprehension of mental health at the time. It was very much the British stiff upper lip approach to weakness: Suck it up and carry on, what are you complaining about, it could be worse, I'm doing it so what's your excuse? It was deemed a weakness to admit that you were struggling, but I know now that that is simply not true. It is the complete opposite.

But at the time, I was burdened with issues that were too much for me to handle, and I did not feel that I had the right to burden others with my problems (problems that I thought I had created for myself). I was distant, moody, and temperamental. I would constantly argue with family and friends and snap at the smallest criticism. I was sick of hearing the same comments from people who meant well but did not understand what I was going through. Being told that other people are dealing with worse, or that things will get better, or that you will get there eventually—it will all work itself out. All these things just felt empty and unhelpful. How do you know that things will get better? What does it matter what other people have experienced?

I spent every day trying to avoid eye contact with other people. I didn't want them to know I was struggling, and I was afraid of breaking down into tears in public. I was too afraid to even look at myself in the mirror because I would often start to cry. I would even try to wear clothes that would help me to blend into the background. I would try my best to avoid attention or interaction; anything that might lead to an angry outburst or a flood of tears. I was constantly on edge and I was exhausted.

The first real moment of relief didn't materialise until much later that year when a colleague of mine, Craig, mentioned his plans to travel across the U.S in passing. He was someone I only saw occasionally during the university breaks and we had always got on, but we didn't really know each other. Nevertheless, after expressing my jealousy of his plans and my dreams of traveling, he didn't hesitate to extend an invitation to me. I thought he was just being polite, but he was serious. I so wanted to say yes, I needed a break; I needed an adventure. And to be honest, I needed to be reminded that I could be happy and that I was allowed to enjoy my life. Being British or just being me, I felt compelled to politely decline Craig's offer even though every part of my being wanted to escape the miserable world I had created for myself. Thankfully, my stepdad encouraged me to go. He knew I needed a break. That was the first sign I picked up on that perhaps people had noticed that things weren't going so well. It was just the little push I needed.

Those two months backpacking across North America were two of the best months of my life. I was able to free myself of my misery and my burden and allow myself to just be me. It was the first time in months I felt relaxed. I felt in control of my choices, and I began to feel like myself again. Craig became one of my closest friends, and he taught me to be a little more selfish; to put myself first sometimes. I began the trip being very accommodating and flexible because I thought that I could only do things we both wanted to do. I compromised on a couple of things that I didn't need to. I didn't mind because I was still happy to be out experiencing life, but after a few weeks, I realised that even though we were travelling together, we could still be independent. Craig also encouraged me to be a little more confident in myself.

I owe so much to that trip because I gained some of the experiences I had missed out on in university. I learnt to be independent, I gained a little bit of confidence, and I discovered my passion for travel and adventure. Plus, I gained memories and stories that will last me a lifetime. But it didn't "cure" me. Don't get me wrong, I was heading down a dark and lonely path, and it certainly saved me in the short-term, but I hadn't yet faced or resolved any of my real issues.

When I came back home, I bounced around a few jobs trying to figure out what I wanted to do. After a couple of years or so, I stumbled across a career. During those years I had many ups and downs, but there were certainly more happy moments than before. Craig had gone on to complete his degree and then headed of on a gap year to Australia. My plan was to join him, but I stumbled upon a job that offered a potential career. I decided to sacrifice my working holiday visa to fix my CV and to build a future for myself.

It was a low-level position, much lower than everyone else my age (they had completed their degrees and jumped straight in at graduate level). Instead, I found myself on £12k a year, still living at home with my parents. But I had to start somewhere.

The job offered hope for a brighter future, but I was always frustrated with being in a position that I felt was too far below where I should have been for my age and my skill set. But you have to prove yourself; you have to follow the corporate path and earn your stripes.

I worked hard, determined to prove myself worthy of a graduate-level job and higher, but a year or so into my new job, the recession hit. Just my luck. At least that was how I felt. Even though millions of people were affected, I couldn't help but think of my own situation. I was already facing years of slow progression, and then this happens. The recession halted my progress by a few more years and added to my stress and anxiety levels. Depression was creeping back with a vengeance. Little did I know it had never really left.

I found myself going through the same process of negativity (thinking if I had just earned my degree then this would not have happened). I would have been earning enough to live away from home. My career would be further ahead, and I could be in Australia with my friend enjoying life to the fullest. All of these ifs, buts, and maybes. I was focusing on the past and still envisioning an empty future for myself. This was going to set me back; I was going to be too old to achieve anything by the time I'd break through this barrier. At this point, I had put so much pressure and importance on reaching a graduate-level position that the barriers to overcome my missing degree began to feel insurmountable once again. I envisioned an invisible glass ceiling that I could not break through. And the more months that passed, the more its importance weighed on me.

When I was driving home along that winding country road contemplating suicide, I imagined what might happen if I were to die. Who would miss me? Who would raise the alarm? Who would visit me in the hospital or come to my funeral? I thought about how I would be remembered. I suffered that journey many times, for weeks on end.

I was seriously considering whether suicide was a sensible option. Could I go through with it? Was it worth continuing if this was how life felt? What would I miss out on if I did? How would my family and friends feel? If anything, those thoughts kept me alive. I wasn't thinking about money or success, I was thinking about the lives I had touched and how I still had more to offer. I felt that I wasn't done yet; I had plenty of things that I wanted to do and things I still wanted to accomplish. I couldn't give in, no matter how much I wanted the pain to end. I had to keep going; for my family, for my friends, but mostly for me. I had to keep fighting.

As the recession began to ease, I found myself craving freedom and adventure. Fortunately, my work offered a sabbatical scheme, and at this point in time, they were open to people taking a break from work to avoid having to let anyone go. I saw it as an opportunity for me to take another break and recharge my batteries once again. I worked overtime with a new sense of purpose to save up enough money to take at least four months off from work and from my ordinary life. I sacrificed spending money on junk food and alcohol for several months to help save up enough money to give me the absolute freedom I craved. I spent my days researching my dream trip, planning which places I wanted to visit, where I would stay, how I would get from A to B, and of course, I had to plan my budget. It gave me purpose and drive once again.

I wanted to visit Australia to do a version of the trip I had imagined years before (the one I sacrificed for my career). I decided to visit Thailand, Kuala Lumpur, and Singapore to break up the journey on my way to Australia. From there, I would head on to New Zealand and finally Fiji. At least, that was the original plan. But along the way, I learnt to be more flexible, and my plans changed somewhat as I went on.

This four-month oceanic adventure was just what the doctor would have ordered. It was certainly challenging travelling alone. I definitely had my low moments as well as my highs, but once again it helped me to grow as a person. It gave me valuable life experience instead of spending five days a week in an office, putting up with office politics and relying on others to help me to learn and progress, ultimately repeating the same weeks over and over. I experienced different cultures and new perspectives. I tested myself to survive in difficult situations; to navigate foreign countries and foreign languages. I met new people from all over the world and put myself out there, outside of my comfort zone on a daily basis. Once again, I found new levels of confidence and self-assurance. I had the time to reflect and to think about what I wanted from life. I pushed my boundaries and ticked off bucket list items that I had previously feared would never be experienced.

I came home having learnt some valuable lessons on life and about me as a person. I began to understand my strengths and weaknesses. I began to consider different perspectives and points of view; to put myself in other people's shoes and to learn from them too. I grew up quite a lot, and I began to feel like a functioning adult. I came back with the absolute goal of making my dream of living in London a reality. The moment I got back to work, I told them of my desire to move to London, and I made it clear that I would do whatever it takes to make it happen. From the moment I was told it would be possible, I did not let up until it happened. I made sure that I got my transfer. Even if it meant moving without getting the promotion I deserved, I would at least get paid enough to survive. In hindsight I may have underestimated just how expensive London can be, but I made it happen nonetheless.

Moving to London didn't solve my problems, but it did feel like progress. At times I was genuinely happy, but I was still fighting an uphill career battle, and my low income made having a happy home and social life a difficult challenge. But I never stopped trying. London can be a cold and lonely place if you let it, but I worked hard, both professionally and personally, and I eventually started to build what felt like a respectable adult life. But still, I faced the same mental health issues. I still had my ups and my downs. There were periods when I felt lonely and periods when I felt that I would never progress my career to a level where I would be satisfied and I could live somewhat comfortably.

I remember sitting on the tube (the London Underground) on my way home from work one day. Having worked a long day, I was tired. Tired from the day and tired from the days and the weeks and the months of doing the same thing, at the same level, with no reward. Working hours and hours, as much as 60 hours a week, I was emotionally drained. I was trying to stay positive and to save face in front of my colleagues; trying to keep it together.

That day on the train, I was listening to music on my headphones. This was something I did when I felt the demons bubbling up inside; the anger and frustration of feeling helpless. I still did not feel comfortable talking about my feelings and continued to suffer in silence.

Mental health was still not a common term in society. Sometimes, the fire inside me would threaten to erupt and I had to fight to keep myself from saying something that might offend or upset someone—an outburst that might cost me my job and my future. I hadn't realised it, but every year that went by felt like another year behind where I should be. The anger and frustration at my powerless position continued to grow inside my mind. Music would help to drown it out momentarily; gangster rap or heavy rock music played on full volume.

That day, I was on my way home trying not to cry; trying to keep it together. My headphones were on full blast as I was trying to drown out my negative thoughts. The lady who was sitting next to me tapped me on my shoulder and expressed her concern for the health of my ears. Her father was a doctor and she warned me of the damage I might be doing, but she had no idea of the pain that I was already feeling. I turned the music down because I hadn't even thought of how it could be impacting others; I was trapped inside my own world just trying to survive. I still had no idea if anyone else was feeling this way or why I was struggling so much. Even when I would make some progress in my life, it would feel like something would go wrong or go against me.

It always felt like two steps back to go one step forward, and this life I had envisioned was always just out of reach: a mountaintop behind yet another false horizon.

It took me a long time to understand what I was actually going through and that it was normal; I was not the only one. It also took me a long time to realise that a lot of the pressure I was feeling, I was putting on myself, and that I needed to find a way to deal with my emotions better. I had to learn to accept them, to talk about them, and to find ways to process them. I desperately needed to work on myself; to start a healing process that would last and better prepare me for the future.

Acceptance

It is the most obvious thing I could possibly write, and you have probably heard it a million times before, but I cannot stress this enough: Admitting you have a problem is the most important step to start your recovery. But self-reflection is not easy, especially when it means admitting that you are not in control of your own thoughts or feelings. We are always so conscious of our outward trajectory that we never focus closely enough on our internal well-being, even though this is where we draw our strength from. This is scary because we convince ourselves that admitting we have a problem suggests that we are weak. Not to our friends or our family, but to ourselves. We question ourselves; why can't I cope with this? Am I not strong enough? No one else seems to struggle, so why do I? What is wrong with me?

Absolutely nothing. There is nothing wrong with feeling like this. It is natural, but it should not be all-consuming. We need to consider how strong we really are. If we can be honest with ourselves and admit that we have a problem and face it, then we have an inner strength that cannot be ignored. It is enigmatically brave. It is far from weak. And, as annoying as this sounds, we are stronger than we give ourselves credit for.

I know this from first-hand experience. Admitting to myself that I was suffering from depression was the last thing I ever wanted to do. I felt weak. I felt like a man from my background, with my attributes, experience, and general situation in life, was not justified in feeling this way—especially when there were others out there with far worse problems than my own. But we are all human beings, and we all have our own battles.

Our brains are incredible things, but they are also very complicated, and the more and more things we must deal with in life, the more complicated they become. Congested, confusing, and tiring. If you spend every day battling within yourself, you won't have the energy to make the changes you need to make. You'll be too worn out from overthinking, stress, and emotional expenditure. You can start to feel trapped inside of yourself. The only way to break free is to face it head-on.

I can't remember a specific moment that this happened, but when I was finally able to make this admission to myself, that was the moment I really and truly accepted that I had a problem. That was the moment that I started to learn to live with it in a more constructive way. I began to take control of my life. I began to implement changes to ensure that I would never let it win. It would not consume me.

It takes time to truly accept what you're going through, but every day it gets a little more obvious and harder to ignore. And when you finally recognise it, you wonder how you hadn't noticed it before. But when you're in the thick of it, you get so caught up with all of these negative feelings that your only goal is to keep it together and to not let anyone see you struggle; to just get through each day as it comes. That is no way to live. It is a horrible way to live. Frustrating. Upsetting. Constantly worrying about everything that is wrong. And seeing no end in sight can be terrifying. It just exacerbates everything. You can be so caught up in this negative cycle of dark thoughts that you really don't have the energy for anything else. But the more you start to read up about it and the more you listen to others who have experienced similar things, the more easily you can see the clouds beginning to disperse.

The more you pay attention to what you're feeling and why, the clearer it becomes that this isn't ok. You've found yourself to be in a tough place; a situation you need to change. Because the harsh truth is, the longer we leave it, the worse it will get. We must act. We must treat it. We don't want to give up without a fair fight. And when we realise that we reach a point of change. A turning point.

Acknowledging your own and very real struggle allows you to identify the specific issues you're facing. This in turn facilitates your acceptance. Once you accept it, you can start to work on it. It is important to understand that you may not be able to fix everything right away, but you will start to make things a lot easier for yourself. We have the power to change a lot more than we think, we just have to go about it the right way. Little by little. Rome was not built in a day; of course not. It takes professional builders a long time to build one house, let alone an entire city, but no matter how many setbacks, they almost always get there in the end, one job at a time.

Life is the same. We can only address one problem at a time. It may take patience, persistence, and perseverance, but you will get there. With every little step, you start to build a stronger foundation.

They say the definition of insanity is repeating the same thing over and over and expecting different results. So, doing nothing has consequences. Continuing along the same path will get you nowhere because nothing will change. Survival is all about evolution; adapting to your surroundings and making changes to survive and thrive. I spent a lot of time dreaming about being saved. Waiting and hoping that fate would intervene. That I'd be struck with a moment of luck or good fortune (something movie-worthy). But that isn't how life works, and when I figured that out and accepted it (that not only do I have a problem but that it will take hard work and time to change my situation), that is when I started to rebuild my life. I understood that it would be hard and that sometimes I would fail. But I would learn, I would persist, I would succeed. Little by little. Things would get better.

Now don't get me wrong, I didn't suddenly find positivity overnight, but I now knew what I was dealing with: depression, anxiety, loneliness. I understood that this wasn't new; that I wasn't the only one. I knew that I could now find a way to make it better. I started to believe in myself again. I was now motivated by the hope of change; there was now a light at the end of the tunnel. I could actually get out of this darkness and start to enjoy my life more. And I did.

The day I turned 30 is the day that I decided to fight back and take control of my mental health. No longer was

I going to let the negativity win. It was time for me to get myself together and make a better life for myself.

This pivotal moment in my life did not happen overnight. I had been working up to it for a while. I had been observing my own behaviour—my thoughts, my feelings, and the actions that I was taking. It began to dawn on me that something wasn't right. Mental health was getting more attention in society and people were starting to talk more openly about it. I began to accept that I had been suffering from depression and anxiety for a long time. Understanding and accepting that made it so much easier for me to work on it. I finally began to understand why I had been struggling and what I had been feeling over the last 10 years or so. With my 30th birthday approaching, I made a bold and brave admission to myself. I decided that it was time for me to open up about my struggle and to let the world know what I had been dealing with. I was maturing, and the milestone of 30 marked a shift in my mental attitude. I was feeling better within myself; I was in a good place.

On the day of my birthday, I made an announcement via Facebook (my virtual mountain top) to inform all my friends and family that I had been suffering with depression for more than a decade. I decided to share an article along with my post, which at the time I felt best reflected much of what I had been experiencing over the years. The article helped me to articulate what the word "depression" actually meant. It depicted many of the feelings and experiences that I had gone through at one time or another. This was important because mental health was still a relatively new topic and I felt that simply saying I had suffered was not enough. I still thought that it would be an alien concept to many people. I wanted to break the taboo. I wanted to let them all know that I was now aware that there was something wrong, even if they hadn't noticed, and I was ready to start talking about it. I was actively encouraging them to talk to me about it. It was a way for me to say ok, this is no longer off-limits, I am open and ready to talk about my mental health.

I was very surprised at the reaction my post received. My intention was to show my friends and family that I was ready to start talking about it and that I was ready to start the healing process. I did hope that my honesty might encourage others to talk more about their feelings too, but I had no idea how many people would relate to me on this matter. I didn't know what to expect when I posted it, but what I got was a lot of comments and messages encouraging me and even congratulating me for my bravery. So many people reached out to me to tell me that they had experienced or were currently going through similar struggles. Some of these really surprised me, partially because of the stigma that was associated with these things and partially because I had no idea those people were also struggling. I think that is when I realised just how common it was. For the first time, I really understood that I wasn't alone and that there wasn't something about me that was uniquely flawed.

I know now that mental health issues are non-exclusive and can often affect all of us in different ways, at different times in our lives. But at the time I was surprised to hear that some of my friends were struggling too—friends who I thought to be confident, self-assured, and outgoing; traits that I had been jealous of and never would have associated with struggles of any kind. But my misconceptions were immediately exposed for me to see. Most of the time we have no comprehension of what people are really thinking or feeling. This day did not only mark the moment that I began to heal, but it created a mental switch from suffering to healing. It also sparked a desire for me to understand more, to read more about the subject, to reflect more on my own journey, and to be more conscious of the journey of others.

The response to my raw honesty was overwhelmingly positive. I spoke about my struggles with mental health in an open and inviting manner for the first time in my life, and I kind of wished I'd had the courage and the strength to do it sooner. It wasn't easy to reach that point in my life, but it was a crucial turning point that was essential to my healing. I had benefitted a lot from the growing public focus on mental health and the increased discussions around it. It had helped me to start to understand what I was suffering with, but it was the response from my friends, people I knew, that really made it sink in. This is a very real and very human problem to have. The most meaningful response I received was probably from one of my closest friends who I'd known for a long time. He told me that he was proud of me for speaking out. He understood how hard it must have been for me to reach that point, and hearing that meant a lot to me. As men, we rarely talk openly about our feelings with other men, and that was especially true for me up until that point. But it was time for that to change.

From that day on, things began to change. It felt like I was gaining more control over my life. I wasn't cured, but it became a little easier to face my struggles. I was now able to put a name to it, and I didn't have to try as hard to hide it. I now had the option to tell my friends if I was having a bad day, and I could admit my feelings to myself instead of ignoring them or bottling them up.

The Four Pillars

Identifying, accepting, and communicating my struggles with mental health helped to give me a new perspective. Instead of feeling like I was drowning and struggling to keep my head above water, I felt like I now had time to breathe and to reflect.

I identified four core pillars in my life that play a pivotal role in my happiness. Identifying these allowed me to almost segment my life, making it easier for me to focus on the things that are not working and to identify the best ways to address them. It also helped me find some security in my mental health because it gave me something to focus and work on instead of feeling lost. As long as I worked hard to sustain at least one of these pillars, I could keep myself together, remain hopeful, and focus my energy on the other areas of my life.

The Four Pillars are my Home Life, Work Life, Social Life, and Love Life. These are the four areas that make up my everyday life; the four areas that I have some degree of influence over.

Your **Work Life** is something you can always work on, whether you change job role, team, location, or employer. Whether you take on new responsibilities, learn a new skill or go independent; you have a lot of choices. But sometimes you may also need to accept that there may be a steep climb to reach your goals, and your patience may be tested. For me, my work life represented a particular pain point in my early adult life, and dropping out of university certainly sparked the hardest period of my depression. For many years afterwards, I struggled with my expectations versus my reality. For years I felt like I was behind in my career, and I had to put my head down and grin and bear it. It was very trying, and it took a toll on my mental health for a long time. But I stuck with it because I believed that I was heading in the right direction. I had to learn to accept that I didn't have complete control over my career and that I needed to learn to play the part and swallow my pride in order to navigate my way up the corporate ladder.

During this time, I chose not to make drastic changes. The world was dealing with a recession, and so I had to learn to be patient. But I was able to give myself reasonable targets, and if I was working towards a promotion, I would speak to my manager and my team and ask them for advice; let them know my intentions and use their help and guidance to achieve my goal. Struggling in silence only makes things feel worse, and we are fortunate to live in a time that gives us so many options and opportunities.

After university I tried my hand at three or four different jobs: I tried hospitality and accountancy, and I eventually found a job in market research. These days it is getting easier and easier to expand your learning and your skill set from your own home, to try new things, and to find your passion. Working remotely or as a freelancer is also becoming more common, and corporate working environments are changing. Being stuck in a dead-end job with no other options is becoming less common, as we now have more choice and control than ever before.

But it is still going to be challenging. There is a lot of competition out there, and finding the right job can take time. Being honest with ourselves, patient, and open-minded can help us to deal with any rejection or failure that we experience along the way. Focus on the progress you are making and change the things you can control.

Now further on in my career, I feel more secure taking risks, but it can still be daunting. Yet I know how important finding the right job can be. Being happy or content in your job is important because it can give you purpose. Your work life makes up a huge part of your adult life, so you shouldn't let yourself struggle for too long. If you are unhappy in your job, you owe it to yourself to change it.

No matter which pillar of your life you are wanting to change, it is only you who has the power to change it. You cannot rely on fate to intervene or wait for a miracle to happen; it is down to you to find the strength to make the necessary changes in your life.

Your **Home Life** is your base. Whether you live by yourself, with your partner, your family, friends, or with strangers, your home is where you eat, rest, and sleep, and this plays an important role in your mental health. Much like your work life, you can't have control over every aspect of your home life. But one would hope that you have some say or influence over it, and this may increase over time as you get older. I lived with my parents until I was 25. It was hard; being a young man full of intent and ambition but having so little freedom. I had a low salary and very few options, and I was lucky enough to have a loving parents to look out for me. But I found it hard during my depression to be at home at that age. I wasn't ready to talk about my mental health, and I had ambitions that I was desperate to pursue.

After my sabbatical backpacking around Asia and Australia, I came back full of vigour and I sat down with my manager at work to ask for a transfer to London. It was time. I was ready for a change, and I knew that I needed to change both my work and home environments. I had to be patient for almost a year, and I worked hard, but I always had this goal in mind. I had given myself hope; something to aim for. A real marker of change and progress. Making a big change like where you work or where you live can be both empowering and unsettling at the same time. Living as an independent adult brings new challenges. In my case, I swapped living with my parents for living with strangers. Shared housing is common in many big cities, and living with strangers can be a bit of a lottery, but I now had more control and more say over who I lived with, where I lived, and how I lived.

Over the years I have changed housemates, apartments, and cities, making subtle improvements each time. I've learnt to enjoy the positives more and to let go of some of the negatives by accepting what is inside of my control and what is not. Living with strangers will do that for you; you have to learn to coexist, which means compromise. This means accepting that you are not perfect and that you are all trying to accommodate each other.

So, I learnt to focus on the positives, like the one housemate I have a good relationship with, or how comfortable my room is, or the fact that I am saving money instead of spending it all on rent. And, if I find myself struggling to see the positives and feeling unhappy or uncomfortable in my own home, I will start to consider whether I can change it. I won't just accept things anymore if I am unhappy. If I have the power to change something, I will, because I know just how important my own happiness is.

It hasn't been easy. I have had some terrible housemates, and when I look back at my first house in London compared to the more recent places I've called home, I can definitely see the progress. My first house was opposite a busy hospital entrance with noisy neighbours, inconsiderate housemates, and a mouse problem. I've made plenty of sacrifices and compromises, but I've always made sure that I felt safe and comfortable enough in my own home. This gives me one less thing to worry about and allows me to focus on other areas of my life.

For me, your home life and your work life are the two most important areas of your life that have a big impact on your mental well-being. It is really important to feel safe and comfortable in your own home because it is your base and your life is always built around it. Your work life is also significant because it occupies a large portion of your time. If you do identify a need to change one or both of these areas like I did, you have to make a conscious commitment to do everything possible on your part to make it happen, whilst also being patient and understanding that big changes take time.

Your **Social Life** is all about enjoying life. Life is hard—at times very hard—but we need to make time to enjoy life as much as we can. We can sometimes get caught up in the grind of trying to build a strong career, or we can focus too much on other issues that take up the majority of our time and energy. But finding time to be social isn't about sacrificing your time; it is an investment into you and your life. Spending time with other people, people you love and whose company you enjoy, gives you strength. We find comfort and support in others, and we are more likely to let go of our stresses, even if only for a short while, to laugh, to smile, to have a rewarding conversation, to enjoy affection, to have fun and enjoy life.

Making time for friends and family is always worth it. You gain so much more from having those moments in your life than you ever will without them. Enjoying life with our loved ones is always more rewarding than being alone, focusing on our careers, worrying about money, and everything else that tries to get in the way. At the end of the day, the only things you will remember are the special moments spent with your loved ones.

When I was struggling with feeling depressed, lonely, or stressed, I often tried to hide myself from the world. I would bury my head in the sand and hope that it would all pass, wishing away my life. But when I started to pay more attention to my mental health, I realised that my social life played an important part in my health and happiness. It was something I looked forward to. Spending time with my friends and family reminded me that I was loved; it reminded me that I had something meaningful in my life.

Your social life is a big part of your life's enjoyment. When you're feeling low, retreating to your home or your room can feel safe; it feels easier somehow. But really, you should be making more of an effort than usual to be around friends and family. In these moments we need to put ourselves out there and make an effort to be with other people to remind ourselves of the joys of life.

During some of my toughest times living in London, when I was living in cheap accommodation, away from my friends, I often felt isolated and alone. Spending all day in bed watching movies and eating comfort food felt safe, but all I was doing was avoiding the issue. I wasn't helping or healing anything. When I realised this, I started messaging and contacting my friends and family more. I wanted to feel more connected. I wanted to talk about what I was feeling and what I was dealing with, but I also wanted to talk about something that wasn't about me and my life. I wanted to be reminded of the world.

I started putting in more effort, inviting my friends out, going for dinner or a walk, or just meeting for a chat. I knew that I needed to see someone; I needed to not be alone. I began to understand the real importance of friendship.

Your good friends will be there for you when you need them. They will lift you up when you are down. Just being able to talk about my problems, even for a moment, helped relieve some of the pressure I was feeling.

Having all this emotion and negative energy bottled up inside is tiring; it drains your energy and ruins your thirst for life. If you are not careful, the days and weeks can turn into months or years of misery. And nobody wants to look back and think, I wish I had tried a little harder.

Time is something we can't get more of, so even when things are hard, we need to try and find as many moments of joy as we can. It isn't easy to pick yourself up when you're feeling low, but something as small as messaging with friends, even if the conversation is short, can feel good. It can help to lift your mood and remind you that there is positivity out there; it isn't all doom and gloom. We just need to look a little harder and push ourselves in the right direction.

I always make an effort to work on my social life. It is always changing. When I moved to Barcelona, I didn't really know anyone, and I knew that if I wanted to meet people and make new friends, I would have to be the one to make an effort. For example, I made sure that every week for the first few months I would try to attend a community social or networking event. I set myself goals and targets and pushed myself each time to get out of my comfort zone and meet new people. It wasn't easy, but as soon as you make a connection, you understand why it is worth it.

One day, my housemate invited me to go to the beach and join his friends, but I wasn't feeling in the mood. But I knew I needed to push myself to get out and meet people, so I said yes to his invite. I ended up making a friendship that became very important to me and one that improved my social life no end. If I had let my anxiety win, we would never have met.

It is important to continually push yourself and not to give up. You have to keep putting yourself out into the world because it's the only way you'll experience it.

Your **Love Life** is another important pillar of your life and your happiness. It really depends on your circumstances, but I think this one is a little harder to control. I often prioritise the other pillars first, but it can play a big role in your life. Whether you find love at a young age or later in life, your love life can offer a lot of fulfilment and happiness. And so can all the flirting, romance, and excitement in-between.

The thrill and excitement that you get from dating, from meeting new people and making connections, are morale-boosting and confidence-boosting. It feels good to be acknowledged and appreciated by someone of interest. And when you find genuine chemistry with another person, it gives you a visceral feeling inside. It awakens your nervous system and makes you feel alive.

Having an active sex life as an adult is a positive thing; it is natural and we sometimes need it. We need to feel the closeness and intimacy that comes with sex. It is a natural stress release; it helps us to relax, gives us confidence, and improves our mindset. Our bodies release dopamine from sex, which boosts our mood and our motivation for life. But it isn't just sex that makes us feel good or reminds us that we are alive. So does romance; even just the excitement of meeting someone new with all the nerves and anticipation that goes along with it.

It is hard to pursue a healthy love life when you are feeling low on confidence or self-esteem. But, putting yourself out there and meeting new people can give you a sense of confidence and help to improve your outlook. It can help you to find positivity more quickly.

A healthy love life is good for all of us. It is the part of our lives that helps us to connect to another human being on a deeper and more meaningful level. Finding comfort and companionship is motivating, encouraging even. Learning to open yourself up to someone and sharing your true self helps to strengthen your inner core. It strengthens your connection with yourself and gives you a stronger belief in others.

Learning to become 'us' rather than 'me' is a positive skill to learn. And having someone else to think about rather than focusing on ourselves helps to alleviate the pressure we put on ourselves, helping us to appreciate life more.

Love is something that we all benefit from, but it cannot only happen if we are active in the world. It is the area I have always found the most challenging, because if you want to meet people, date them and be intimate, there is no hiding from your anxiety or your low self-confidence. The only way to achieve a fulfilling love life is to face those issues head-on. This is why I first focused on building up a strong home life as my base; my stable rock in my life. Then I worked on improving my work life and my social life before I tried to really push forward with my love life. Improving the other pillars of my life first gave me a much stronger foundation to rely on. It gave me the strength to step outside of my comfort zone more often and to deal with my anxiety.

A Healthy Body Fuels a Healthy Mind

In my late 20s whilst living in London, I started to realise that whenever I felt depressed, I found myself seeking comfort in food and isolation. I would hide away from the world, spending my evenings and weekends watching movies and being lazy at home on my own. I would often end the night with comfort food accompanied by a sad film.

I was avoiding social contact; I felt too emotionally vulnerable to be with friends, and I didn't want to be the one who brought down the mood of the evening. I didn't want to be a burden. It was a way for me to justify staying at home and to make myself feel better. I'd eat whatever I wanted, I slept a lot, and I spent a lot of time indoors away from fresh air and sunlight. As a result, my skin would break out, I would become even more self-conscious, and my desire to stay at home and hide away would become even greater. I would pick and scratch at the imperfections in my skin, which only made things worse, but I was angry, frustrated, and agitated with the way that I felt. I would scrutinise my appearance in the mirror over and over. I was essentially causing minor harm to myself, which only gave me more of a reason to hide myself away from the world.

It was a horrid, bitter cycle. I would sleep no end, sleeping until midday on weekends, trying to avoid being seen by anyone. I'd even wear a hoodie while out in public to try and hide as much of my face as possible. I just didn't want to be seen or judged by anyone. I just wanted to fade away.

If I drank alcohol, I would drink too much. I wasn't taking care of myself, and instead of making the situation easier, I was making it worse. I was low on energy, enthusiasm, and self-confidence. I began to notice that whenever I ate badly, I was usually feeling down and depressed. It took me a while to realise it, but the way I was living was making the situation worse. The food I was eating, the lack of exercise, the lack of sunshine and fresh air, was taking its toll on my mind and my body.

But I was tired of being tired. And I decided that I'd had enough of missing out on life and avoiding social situations. Although I couldn't bear to see anyone in the moment, deep down I wanted to be out and about, having fun with friends rather than hiding away at home, alone.

So I started to make changes to my diet. I forced myself to cook my own meals more regularly and avoid using any fast food or delivery services. I made sure that I was getting more fruit and vegetables in my diet. I made sure that I was going to the gym after work at least three or four times a week to get some exercise. I needed to work off some stress and to make myself feel like I had accomplished something for myself each day.

On the weekends I set my alarm to remind myself that I was no longer hiding away; I needed to get out of bed and make more of the day. I made sure that even if I didn't socialise with anyone, I would at least go for a walk and get some fresh air and sunshine. You don't realise just how important it is to breathe fresh air and the positive impact sunlight has on your mood. Locking yourself away in your home may feel safe and comfortable, but we need to be outdoors, and we need to be more active, otherwise our bodies begin to shut down.

The moment I started eating better and exercising regularly, I started to see an improvement within myself. Each day it got a little easier for me to wake up in the morning and face the day. After cutting out so much salt and fat from the fast foods, my skin began to heal. I felt less afraid to be seen in public, and I was less likely to avoid interacting with other people. I became less self-conscious of my appearance and I began to speak to other people more rather than isolating myself (and amplifying the feeling of loneliness). I stopped trying to avoid eye contact so much, and eventually, as I began to feel healthier and more confident, I became more comfortable with it.

It did not take long to see improvements, and after a little while I started to notice the bigger impact on my lifestyle change. I began to feel more positive about things in general. I began to make more of an effort to see my friends, and I started to have a life again. It wasn't all doom and gloom anymore; there were more moments of positivity.

It was not a miraculous cure, but something as simple as changing my diet, getting outside into the real world more, and getting a little more exercise began to give me my energy and strength back. I began to feel more comfortable in my own skin again, and I was in a better mental state to deal with things.

They say that misery loves company, but I say depression loves isolation, and the worst thing you can do is to close yourself off from the world. Do not give in to the temptation to hide yourself away. Find comfort in nature and fuel your mind and body with a healthy diet and plenty of exercise.

I realised that too much sugar, salt, and fat was negatively adjusting my mental chemistry. It was like I was poisoning my mind, starving myself of positive energy. So, I cut out the fast food, the crisps (chips), the cakes, chocolate, ice cream, and even the readymade meals too. I started eating healthy recipes. Every meal contained fruit or vegetables, and I expanded my home cooking recipe list.

I reached a place in my life where I began to understand the importance of 'balance.' If I want to eat comfort food from time to time, I need to eat healthy the rest of the time to balance it out. If I want to enjoy a lazy day occasionally, I need to make sure I am making the effort to be active regularly too. And I won't let work take over my life either. Working long hours disrupts your diet and your exercise routine too much, which is too much of a sacrifice in terms of health. So, I started pushing back at work and demanding a better work-life balance. I needed to make sure that I was getting enough rest and that I get to enjoy a part of the day for myself too, whether it be exercise or dinner with friends. Finding balance gave me more control over my life and it made me feel much better about it. I felt much less guilty if

I indulged in a rare treat, and I felt more positive about the way I was living. It made a big impact on my mood.

I would always encourage anyone struggling with their mental health to review their current lifestyle, their diet, and their exercise routine. And I would advise you to steer clear of diet plans because they are just short-term solutions; they just don't last. A lifestyle change is a long-term commitment to the way that you live your life, not just a temporary solution. It takes a lot of effort and commitment, but it is worth it. If it is affecting your mental health then it needs to be a change that you keep for good, to make sure you are giving your mind and your body the support needed to deal with the stresses of life.

I now make meals using natural ingredients as much as possible, avoiding sugars and preservatives. And although I'm not a vegan, I do try to limit my intake of meat because my body does not need as much as I used to eat; it was a little excessive and a waste of money. I wanted to find more of a balance, and if I'm reducing my carbon footprint at the same time, then all the better. I aim to eat meat only once a day, and one day a week I'm usually vegetarian too to mix it up but also to ensure I'm not overeating. I tend to eat red meat only once a week at most, and I try to get in a mix of fish and other proteins too.

After reading up a lot on health and nutrition, I now know what my Basal Metabolic Rate (BMR) and my Total Daily Energy Expenditure (TDEE) are, roughly. The BMR considers your height, weight, and age, while your TDEE considers how active you are to allow you to tailor your diet to what your specific body needs.

I understand what my daily calorie target is to either maintain, lose, or gain weight, and what proportions of protein, carbohydrates, and fat (macronutrients) my body needs. This means I have a clear understanding of the type of foods I need to get into my meals each day. I compliment these macros with plenty of micronutrients that come from fruit, vegetables, beans, seeds, and nuts. This is something I think we should all learn in school.

Recent studies have shown that most adults are not eating a well-balanced, healthy, and nutritious diet. It isn't easy to achieve the perfect balance, but the more we can do to understand this, the better we can prepare ourselves for the lives that we lead.

It can be a little daunting to overhaul your diet and exercise routine, but there is a lot of information out there. It is just a matter of finding the right source. But there are also plenty of trusted health and exercise apps out there, as well as publications and influencers who can help you to find the right balance to fit your lifestyle. But my mental state is always better when I eat well and stay active, so I cannot recommend it enough. Fuel your body and heal your mind.

Lessons Learned

- Your diet affects your mood and your energy levels. The more sugar, salt, and fat you eat, the more negative emotions you are likely to feel.

- Oversleeping or a lack of sleep can be signs of depression or an unhealthy lifestyle.

- Diets are short-term fixes, not long-term solutions. A balanced lifestyle of healthy eating and regular exercise is crucial for a positive mindset.

- Minimise your intake of sugar, salt, fat, and alcohol.

- Learn your TDEE (Total Daily Energy Expenditure) and eat a healthy balance of macronutrients in your diet.

- Eat plenty of micronutrients every day by including fruit or veg in at least two meals a day.

- Review your current lifestyle and make changes to improve your mental and physical well-being.

- Make home-cooked meals the norm and leave treat meals as just that, occasional treats.

- Set your alarm and give yourself tasks to do each day. Go for walks, see your friends, and keep active.

- Remember, depression loves isolation. Don't let it win.

Excuses

Whether it is a reoccurring theme of procrastination or a perpetual habit of talking yourself out of something, excuses can be an unconscious safety net that we employ regularly without realising it; a parachute that you pull the cord on out of pure habit, allowing you to gently avoid any potential disappointment or heartache. But they can also be a huge hypothetical barrier, constantly blocking your progression or personal evolution. I'm certainly guilty of making regular excuses.

To some extent, I am a realist. I like to take an objective view of things and be honest with myself about the challenges I face and my potential for success. But quite often, I mistake excuses for genuine obstacles. I have a habit of talking myself out of things because deep down, I want to protect myself from getting hurt; to avoid failure or embarrassment. Subconsciously, I put up these walls in my personal and my professional life to protect myself. But I know that if I want to succeed at anything, I must learn to fail. I must learn to take some risks, stop making so many excuses, and just give it a shot. Even if some of those excuses may turn out to be true, you can't know for sure unless you try. And you may discover something in the process.

However, when it comes to our own lives, we can find ourselves focusing too much on the negatives and worrying about the risks involved. It's easy to get used to this way of thinking until it becomes normal and you find yourself stuck in a rut. Playing it safe all the time may help you to protect yourself from some immediate pain or discomfort in the short term, but you might also be preventing yourself from finding a change that leads to more freedom and happiness in the longer term.

I make excuses in all parts of my life, like my love life, for example. I'm always focusing on the 'what ifs': what if she does not like me back or turns me down? An easy excuse to avoid putting myself out there. Or take work, for example. I have told myself numerous times that I am not quite ready to ask for a promotion or that I don't tick all the boxes in the job description, so why even try applying? Excuses can hold you back, and instead of saving you from repercussions, it prevents you from ever experiencing the things you really want. Not because of something you lack or because you aren't good enough, but because you didn't try. Life doesn't just happen. Chance or fate are not going to intervene at the right moment. If you keep making excuses, nothing will change.

Another form of making excuses is selective or motivated reasoning, and I have been guilty of this a few times. This is basically a form of confirmation bias, when your doubts or your fears are looking for a valid argument to support your excuse for not doing something; justifying your natural instinct to protect yourself. This can happen to me when the lines between being realistic with myself and making excuses become blurred, and I end up over-compromising.

Compromise is good because it can help you to find a balance between taking risks while protecting yourself at the same time. This way, you are not overstretching, but by doing so you can often lose out on the full benefits of going all in. Sometimes you just need to take the chance. Sometimes the reasoning you have come to is biased in its nature to protect yourself, and often those reasons can be formed from misinformation or created by fear.

For example, I compromised a lot on my dreams to travel the world. I sacrificed huge parts of my dreams to be pragmatic; to be a sensible grownup. You could argue that reducing the length and journey of my trip to allow me to take a sabbatical from work and stay employed was a smart decision. By not risking my financial security whilst still being able to travel, I made a smart compromise; one that kept my ego in check and allowed me to pursue a part of my dream without taking too much of a risk. But what I've come to learn is that there are no rules on how to live your life, and there are no guarantees, even if you take the safest route. We are bought up to believe that there is a certain way to live your life; a chronological order of things, and it is this way of thinking that really made me struggle in life. I was trying to conform to the normal way of doing things; to fit a mould that is somehow meant to work for everyone. Go to school followed by college and university, then get a job, find a partner, get married, buy a house, have kids, and all this by the time you are 30 years old. Why? We have so many more choices than this. There are a thousand different routes we can take, and we have way more freedom and control than we often realise.

For a long time, I felt the pressure of hitting these milestones in quick succession, and whenever I struggled, I had to battle with myself to fight my instincts to be different; to explore and enjoy life. I reasoned with myself that I needed to have a nine to five job, or that I needed to do things a certain way or act in a certain way. But this is such a destructive way of thinking. It is good to give yourself goals to aim for, but we should not limit ourselves to fit everyone else's way of thinking. This is what happened to me when I was faced with going to university. I wasn't ready for it, but society told me I had to be. So, I panicked under the weight of the expectations I had put upon myself at society's behest. I over-compromised in trying to fulfil my duty and appease expectations.

The reasoning behind those compromises should have been red flags, but I had very little life experience at the time, and I thought I was doing what was right. I was making decisions that I thought would force through the most 'acceptable' outcome and protect myself in the process, but it was always doomed to fail. I forced myself to go to university because the idea of not doing so was terrifying. I was scared of what that would mean for me and my future, but instead, I ended up sinking deep into a full-blown depression and one of the toughest periods of my life.

This is what happened when I was 22 when I gave up my Australian working visa to focus on improving my CV. I reasoned with myself that if I were to take a gap year, my career prospects would only get worse. But that was an assumption that had been passed on to me by society. At that point in time, it was a lot less common to live and work abroad and was, therefore, an unfamiliar concept, and hence the wrong thing to do. Even though travelling through Oceania and living abroad was a dream that I really wanted to fulfil, my conscience took over, and I decided once again that the smart thing to do was to listen to reason and to sacrifice my year abroad for the prospect of a career.

I now know that there is no reason why that trip couldn't have led me to a career or a positive outcome of some kind, because there is not always a right or wrong answer. You never get to see what you could have gained or what you could have lost. But I do know that I can't dwell on the past, and although I talked myself out of that particular dream, I know that I got myself a career out of the decision, and it led me to other great experiences instead.

In the end, my compromise was to do a shorter version of the trip instead, so after a couple of years of stable work, I was able to take a four-month sabbatical and visit Asia and Australia. It wasn't quite the same as what I had envisioned for me, but it was still an incredible and life-changing experience. And, at the time of taking the sabbatical, there was still an element of risk and uncertainty about my future prospects. But I now had some work experience to fall back on.

Playing it safe and doing what I think I am meant to do is something that challenges me every time I am faced with a big decision. I find myself fighting with the urge to avoid it altogether; to procrastinate. Because my desire to take risks is always butting heads with my urge to protect myself, I often find myself making excuses not to do something. I have to remind myself that taking myself outside of my comfort zone is a good thing.

Some of the best things I have ever done in my life were scary, and although they took a little courage and sacrifice, they were more than worth it. Having a conscience and not being completely reckless obviously does have its benefits. It can stop you from taking excessive risks. But we also need to understand what a reasonable fear is and what is ultimately an excuse to play it safe.

This is something I try to ask myself often because I know I have a tendency to be pragmatic, and I also have a stubborn urge to fight comfort and take risks. It is a balancing act that I have to work on because I can't let the excuses win and I can't always play it safe. If I do that, I'll end up sacrificing too much and miss out on life.

I have accepted the reality that I simply can't know what the right choices are, even if there is a 'right' answer. And I don't need to consume myself with the fear of the past. The past is the past. I cannot change it, but I can change my future. I know that I need to learn to trust my instincts a little more and not put so much pressure on myself. We all need to know whose advice to listen to and when, and not to let society dictate how we live our lives.

Applying too much pressure can force us to entertain our doubts and fears, and we can end up over-compromising. Understanding when the reward is worth the risk and having a plan B as your safety net is a better approach than piling up the excuses and talking yourself out of something you really want to do. I have taken my fair share of risks in my life, and the older I get, the more I understand the value of that. Not letting the fear win has led me to some amazing experiences, and who knows what could have happened if I had learnt that lesson earlier on. I may not always get it right, and I may struggle from time to time, but I am not playing it safe. I am finding a balance that works for me.

Lessons Learned

- Excuses are often mistaken for genuine obstacles.

- Selective reasoning uses confirmation bias to accept our excuses and support our fears.

- Excuses, reasoning, and compromise can keep us safe and prevent us from making mistakes, but they can also hold us back. Don't let your anxiety keep you from fulfilling your dreams.

- Playing it safe can be as big a risk as the one you're avoiding taking. Sometimes you need to go all in.

- The social rules and pressures of society are outdated. There are no rules and no guaranteed ways to find happiness. In truth nobody knows what they are doing; we are all just figuring it out as we go along.

- Try not to over-compromise for the sake of others, and don't talk yourself out of something that you really want to do.

- What your parents did may not work for you, and that's ok. Do what is right for you, even if it means breaking the norm and challenging conventions.

- It's ok to take risks in pursuit of what makes you happy.

Emotional Vulnerability

Throughout my early 20s, I was in such denial. I had no idea just how much of a mess I was. I put so much focus on one thing, something that I'd never had, that I honestly believed or even hoped would 'cure' me. I kept thinking that all I needed was a bit of luck. But the longer and longer it went without ever materialising, the more emphasis I put on it and the more of a fable it became. It was endless torment. The love pillar of my life was the one that had always eluded me.

Throughout my teenage years and my early 20s, I genuinely believed that falling in love would solve everything. Meeting a beautiful woman would instantly boost my confidence and remove my depression. But when I finally met a beautiful woman who wanted to be with me, that didn't happen. I was 24 and backpacking across Asia and Australia. On maybe the second day of my trip, I met a beautiful English girl, and we spent a lot of time together. But even though I felt butterflies and I had a smile on my face, deep down it didn't really change how I felt. It was no miraculous cure, as I had naively thought it would be.

Many of the issues I was dealing with had nothing to do with being single or missing out on love. Some of these issues came to light because I now had a real reason to face them. I had met this beautiful woman who filled my heart with excitement, but it also filled my consciousness with dread and anxiety. I was insecure about my lack of both emotional and physical romantic experience. I quickly realised that I was not at all comfortable being vulnerable with someone.

Being intimate with another person was almost alien to me; being naked and exposed. I wasn't a virgin, but I had very little experience at the time. I was still young; I was only 24, and my state of mind was far from someone comfortable and confident with who they were. A part of me was obviously excited by the prospect of love, and the other part of me was terrified of heartbreak. Every time I saw her, she put a smile on my face. When we spent time together, I enjoyed every moment—but not completely.

There was still a part of me that was in turmoil, doubting and second-guessing every move, every thought, every feeling. Should I hold her hand, put my arm around her, kiss her, compliment her? I scrutinised everything. I played out every possible reaction in my mind, and as a result I usually talked myself out of it. I ignored my instincts. I was too scared to ask. Too scared to open up and be honest with her. Perhaps it was too soon to lay it all out there, but keeping it all to myself almost certainly kept me at distance. Surely she noticed something was off. I was constantly aware of it. I couldn't just relax and be myself; be present in the moment and enjoy it. The more time we spent together, the easier it would get, but I still had my walls up, keeping me from ever being myself. I unconsciously confined our relationship to failure before it had even truly begun.

What I needed to do was to be a little more open. I know that now. Had I just found that little bit of courage and spoke about this with her; if I had told her how I felt and had been a little more transparent with my lack of experience and my shaky confidence, things may have turned out a little different. Instead, I was so wound up with anxiety that my stress levels interfered with how I projected myself outwardly. It wasn't just my personality that was inhibited, but also our relationship and my ability to connect emotionally with her. Even the sex was affected.

I put too much pressure on myself; too much expectation, and so the anxiety would take over. I was struggling with low self-esteem and a lack of confidence, and my expectations were therefore misaligned. My anxiety levels were so high that the sex was mostly disappointing for her and uncomfortably stressful for me. Which only made things worse and created more stress. I felt embarrassed and ashamed, and I was too afraid to talk about it. But if I had, I know she would have responded positively. She wouldn't have mocked me or berated me. She might have made me feel more at ease, but my fear took over. I made mountains out of molehills. I let my insecurities and my fears control me. It obviously didn't work out, and at the time I didn't know why. I blamed it on bad fortune and timing. I didn't yet know that I had a lot of work to do on myself.

I hated feeling vulnerable. And for a long time, I was reluctant to let anyone in. Being intimately vulnerable with someone unnerved me. I was always so guarded, subconsciously trying to protect myself from getting hurt.

Over the last few years in my 30s, I have learnt to open up to my friends and I'm quite open about my thoughts and my feelings. But when it comes to dating or romantic intimacy, I am still a little guarded.

More recently I have begun to open up a lot more and I have shown more of myself. I have even shared some of my insecurities with recent lovers. I haven't yet found a partner worth sharing my life with, but previously I was outwardly rejecting it. I was so insecure with myself that it was impossible to find a partner who would have been willing to be patient enough to wait for me to open up naturally. I emotionally distanced myself; I kept myself from becoming too invested, allowing myself to escape unharmed if and when the relationship ended.

When you feel insecure or you are struggling with your mental health, it is hard for you to be comfortable sharing your whole self with another person. It is very scary to allow yourself to feel something; to create an emotional bond with someone who may decide to up and leave in the near future, leaving you with a new wound to heal. It is hard for you to identify your own behaviour as self-destructive, but it is much harder for you to build a deep emotional bond with someone if you are holding back your inner thoughts and feelings, keeping yourself at an emotional distance. Your prospective partner is not going to feel encouraged if you are unable to reciprocate the feelings and the effort that they are putting into the relationship. Over the years I have dated many women who struggled with this entanglement. On one level we would have a connection, but on the other hand, it felt restricted, as though something was missing.

It doesn't feel natural if your partner is sharing intimate details of their life and you are internalising most of yours.

As men, historically we have not been encouraged to talk about our feelings on a deeper level or even show emotion and vulnerability of any kind. I am now at a place in my life where I have no reservations in admitting that I am an emotional man, and I almost always cry at sad films or videos. But I, much like most people, feel deeply self-conscious about crying in public and crying in front of someone you don't yet fully know or trust. It is a difficult conflict of feelings to process. Even just feeling vulnerable, talking about our insecurities, our fears, or our feelings can be unnerving. So much so that the uncomfortable feeling of putting it all out there and being vulnerable whilst we wait for a response is too scary to even process.

Instead, we often tell a lie to avoid it entirely. "I'm fine" is something you will hear almost every day; people too often hide how they are really feeling to avoid the complication and the effort involved in explaining everything in detail. We also want to avoid burdening others with our problems. We will do anything to skip past the conversation as fast as possible to avoid any focus on ourselves, because the thought of telling another human being—no matter how close they are to you—that you are struggling can be terrifying. I avoided it for years. I didn't tell anyone in my life that I was struggling, and it was a horrible feeling. I would avoid eye contact or avoid going out, make excuses, put on a fake smile, or pass off any interest in my life with a sarcastic comment or a bald-faced lie; anything to deflect their attention away from my emotionally vulnerable state.

Sometimes it can feel like no one can really relate to what you are going through. Not fully. Everyone has experienced their own challenges, and it is hard to imagine that life is truly easy for anyone. We are too emotionally complex for that to be true. But even so, when you look around your friends and family, it's natural to wonder if anyone really understands how much you are struggling. But many people do. My public admission on my 30th birthday showed me that, and there has been enough media coverage recently to show that most of us struggle. It is natural to feel alone, but you're not. Let that sink in.

You're not alone in feeling this way; it's natural and normal, so allow yourself to accept that. Learning to be more comfortable with my own vulnerability is something that I have accepted, and it is something I will continue to work on. I know that if I truly want love and a lasting partnership, I will have to learn to share the whole me.

The strongest people are those who are comfortable in their own skin, and the strongest relationships are the ones built on honesty and trust.

Little by little, I have begun to be a bit more talkative earlier on in relationships, sharing more details about my life and talking about my mental health. It makes a big difference for me to understand their receptivity to the matter and for them to see my trust and commitment to building a lasting bond. I am no longer afraid to admit that I have struggled, and if someone shows me that they want to know and to understand what I have been through, then I am willing to share my story. And crucially, I am willing to hear it all too.

I actively encourage, not just lovers but friends also, to share their thoughts and their feelings, especially if I sense hesitation or something deeper to what they are actually sharing. I like to show people that our relationship is a safe space; I will not judge, I am willing to listen, and I am willing to support you. After all, if we want to be comfortable feeling vulnerable with another person, we have to be just as comfortable allowing them to feel as safe with us to do the same.

From the moment I started to talk about my experiences and opened up about my feelings, I started to heal. I can look back now and see the staggering progress I've made since that brave announcement on my 30th birthday. After that point, I let go of a lot of the unrealistic expectations I had previously put upon myself, and I found a new level of confidence. I felt more at ease with who I was as a person, and I began to see my self-esteem and my confidence improve. I put less pressure on my professional and my personal status. I started dating more.

Just before my 31st birthday, I met a girl whose personality was the opposite of mine. She was a very confident, outgoing, and positive person. At first, I was taken aback by her enthusiasm. I didn't think I was ready for it. I was feeling better in myself, but I still had a long way to go, and so I worried about whether I could keep up with her. But I decided to go with it; to believe in myself and to give her a chance. She quickly forced me out of my comfort zone, in a good way. She encouraged me to be more talkative and to open up a bit more. She didn't judge me; in fact, just seeing her so at ease with me, listening to me and not responding negatively, was so empowering. She helped me to feel more comfortable with being more open about my situation, my feelings, and my insecurities. It gave me a much-needed boost. It removed some of the burden I was still carrying, and it allowed my true personality to start to shine through.

Our fears often have a way of manifesting an unrealistic portrayal of life in our own minds. It stops us from taking opportunities we perceive as risks. But a lot of the time, the risk is not real, and people won't judge you or mock you for being honest. And being genuinely open and honest with your feelings is refreshing and often appreciated. It is a brave thing to do; to put yourself out there. But people appreciate it, and it can save you a lot of pain and heartache in the long run.

So, we had some of the most honest and meaningful conversations I have had with anyone in a long time. It was an experience I needed. I stepped outside of my comfort zone and I benefitted from it.

Not only did she help me to open up, but she helped me to find a new level of confidence in the bedroom too. We had the most adventurous and satisfying sex life. I felt more at ease with myself and freer from my usual worries and concerns, so my body was also uninhibited. Instead of brief and disappointing sexual experiences full of anxiety, it was the complete opposite. The sex lasted for hours, and I was able to enjoy every exciting minute of it, free from my interfering anxiety. By not playing it safe; by not shying away from dating and allowing myself to have a genuine and honest conversation, I was able to enjoy life a little more.

My experiences with this woman changed my life for the better. It was just what I needed to keep progressing forward with my mental health. Sex became less of an issue for me. The weight and expectation relaxed into confidence and reassurance. Sex is an important part of any relationship; it allows you to connect on a deeper and more intimate level.

Previously, sex often caused me stress and anxiety, and I allowed it to interfere with my relationships too many times. But now I know the value of being more open with my feelings, not just because it improved my sex life, but because it helps me to feel more at ease and more comfortable being vulnerable. If I can have an honest conversation with someone and feel comfortable with them, then I know I am spending time with the right person.

Your anxiety and stress can be a real burden; they can get in the way of life, so it is not worth spending time with someone who makes it worse. If you feel you have to hide it from them; you have to bottle it up and pretend to be someone you are not, then they are not the right person for you. The best thing you can do in that situation is to be honest and walk away from it. Put yourself first.

This plays a big role in how I choose the women I spend my time with. I want someone who trusts me enough to be honest with me and who respects and supports my choice to open up to her. We must feel comfortable and safe in our relationships. A relationship is something meaningful and lasting. So, choose someone who makes your life better and whose life you also improve. Together you are stronger, not weaker, and if you can't be yourself; if you can't be honest with your feelings, then perhaps it is not a good fit.

When your anxiety or your fears are noticeably affecting your life, changing your personality or getting in the way of you enjoying life, it's time to act. It's time to do something about it. If you want to find love and be happy, it really does start with you. You really can't find love in others if you do not yet love yourself. Working on yourself first means that you are less likely to get in your own way when it matters. Life is hard enough without us putting additional pressure on ourselves.

Lessons Learned

- It is extremely important to talk about your mental health.

- The more you open up to talk about your worries, fears, and insecurities, the easier it will become to face them.

- Speaking about your feelings out loud helps you to process them better.

- We men need to learn to deal with our emotions and not care what others think. The more in tune we are with our emotions, the stronger the man we will be.

- Honest conversations are the ones that matter most.

- Put less expectation on relationships and learn to talk about how you feel early on so you can be comfortable with each other.

- Only be with someone who encourages and supports you to be your whole self.

- Being there for someone else reminds you that you're contributing something positive to those around you.

- Step out of your comfort zone and spend time with people who challenge you in a positive way.

The Consequence
of Loneliness

As a single person, your life can be perceived to be free of responsibility, which implies that you have absolute freedom and control over your life. But in reality, that just isn't true. Through most of my 20s, I struggled with being single, although I tried not to let it hold me back. I embraced my freedom as much as I could, and I have tried to enjoy life as much as possible. I've travelled the world and ticked off many bucket-list experiences. But when seeking adventure and following your dreams as a single person, there is often a choice to make: Either you have to be patient and wait for a friend to become available, or you have to go and do it alone. It depends a lot on your situation, but many of my close friends have either been in relationships and were no longer free for big adventures, or they were not interested in the same types of adventures as I was. Although I have been fortunate enough to have shared a few adventures with friends, I have done most of them alone. I did my first skydive by myself, and when I travelled across Asia and Australia for four months, I went alone.

Going it alone can be an amazing experience, but it can also be a bit daunting, and there will be lonely moments. There are no guarantees, but that is the risk you have to take to avoid missing out entirely. And I would always say it was worth the risk; worth the few lonely nights or uncomfortable moments. I have done a lot in my life, and I am grateful for the experiences that I have created for myself. But it is the ones shared with someone else that mean the most and last the longest. So, it is because of this that I sometimes procrastinate. I make excuses and I put off experiences, big or small, until I can find someone to share them with. But that often means I end up missing out entirely. I put my life on hold for someone or for a moment that does not yet exist in my life.

Having been single for most of my adult life, I have had the freedom to push myself to my limits, to take myself out of my comfort zone, and to pursue my dreams. Being free of the responsibilities and the obligations that come with relationships and raising a family can be great, but it can also be challenging. Without that immediate support network, it can be hard dealing with your mental health alone. Being single has been a particularly difficult challenge for me from time to time. If I am actively dating and meeting people, then I don't worry so much about making that meaningful connection. Or if I am busy working, socialising, and enjoying life with friends and family, spending only a few days or nights alone, then it is easier not to think about it. But when I find myself going through a particularly long period without dating, without a busy social life, or spending too many nights by myself, the loneliness can creep back in. And the longer that feeling persists, the more at risk I am of depression clawing its way back into my life.

After a few months, I would start to focus on the negatives more, feeling alone; feeling empty or unwanted. Like there is a hole or a void inside of me. I grew up believing in love; in fairy-tale romances sparked by chance or serendipity. I am a romantic at heart and a bit of a dreamer, which can make it hard for reality to live up to my expectations.

Now I can see that I gave the idea of love and romance too much emphasis in my mind for too long. I put way too much pressure on myself from a young age to find the right girl and to fall in love. And perhaps I robbed myself of potential romances or experiences because they could never live up to my misguided expectations. I gave myself an impossible task to replicate a fictional life. I believed that I had to find love so that I could be married with a family before I was too old to do so, because that's how society raised me. And the older I got, the harder it became to deal with rejection or to handle those periods of loneliness. I felt the walls of time closing in on me.

When you are single and struggling with loneliness, it can be hard to face life's challenges by yourself. If your mind is not in the right place, it can start to feel like things are piling up and that the universe is against you. We all experience a bit of bad luck from time to time, but now and again it can really catch you by surprise, and it can be difficult to deal with. Dealing with one or two disappointments can be tricky, but when it feels like lots of things are going against you, it can be overwhelming. Especially when you are making a concerted effort trying to do something about it.

It can be easy to lose hope. All the little things suddenly feel much bigger, and all the big things feel insurmountable. I have felt broken on many occasions in my life when I hit such rough patches. It feels like there are no positives in your life, only negatives. And it feels like it is getting worse and you're heading for disaster. The negative thoughts will gather. Why is this happening to me? Why do so many things seem to go against me? Why can't I catch a break? Am I the only one? How am I supposed to find the strength to pick myself up again? I cannot keep feeling like this. I feel lost. I'm scared. I'm lonely. Is it always going to be this way? Am I going to be alone and miserable forever?

No! You cannot think like that.

When this happens, it is important to take a step back and breathe. Your anxiety is taking over and clouding your thoughts. Your fears begin to manifest, and they can feel all too real, but they are just thoughts; just fears. It is natural to feel this way, but it won't last forever, and you can take action against it. When you start to feel like this, try to pay attention to how you are feeling and realise that you need to take action to calm yourself down. Take a walk outside and get yourself some fresh air; try to clear your mind. It's about removing yourself from the negative environment, even if just for a moment. Take some deep breaths and relax your shoulders. Talk to someone about how you feel. Don't fight it.

There was a period in my life when I was living in London in my mid-20s and I was incredibly down, lonely, and unknowingly desperate. I craved intimacy and human contact. I was miserable and spent my days dreaming of a better life, wishing for something or someone to come and save me. I fantasised about a more exciting and fulfilling life, full of meaningful encounters and memorable moments. But it was hard to find the money to fund such ambitions and even harder to galvanise my friends into breaking the normal routine of weekend drinking.

I often went out for a few drinks with friends or colleagues, but the alcohol only made things worse. Regardless, I threw myself into whatever social engagement I could scramble an invite for. Being in London, it was usually at the pub, so every week, once, twice, or more often than not, I was in the pub trying to escape my life; trying to avoid a lonely night at home with my thoughts.

At the start of every working week, I would try to organise plans for the looming weekend ahead. It was a lot of desperate effort to ensure I would not be alone for an entire weekend. The thought of being alone with my thoughts scared me. Inevitably, some weeks I failed to find anyone to join me, and I would end up deliberately working late on a Friday night to avoid going home. Even if it meant being alone in the office, because it felt as though I was delaying the start of the weekend. Somehow, my being there in the office working was better than being at home. But as the office began to fall into silence and darkness, I'd be forced to accept defeat. When you're feeling low, it can be hard to find the motivation to pick yourself up and take yourself out into the world.

It is much easier to go off on adventures on your own when you feel happy and confident. When you're feeling down, the tendency is to hide yourself away and wish for the time to pass more quickly until you find some company or a more positive mindset again.

I found myself drinking more than usual. I would take up every offer to join a social gathering in the pub, even if the last thing I wanted to do was drink. Even if I didn't feel like talking to anyone, I wanted a distraction. Often, I found myself wanting, spending the night longing for a beautiful woman to waltz in and steal my heart away. I had lost sight of my limits and self-control, and I didn't know when to stop. It wasn't dangerous, but it wasn't healthy either. Even when I didn't want to drink anything more or I wanted to go home to bed, I was too afraid too. I didn't feel I had a justifiable reason to leave the social situation and replace it with an empty room of solitude. I didn't know when to leave. I would always find myself as the last man standing; a blurry haze of realisation that my friends have all left and gone home to bed.

I would be in a bar, intoxicated, surrounded by strangers, alone; but I would be too inebriated to notice. I would end up taking a long, slow, and lonely journey home. My drunken state would kick up my emotions, and I'd feel worse than if I'd stayed home in the first place. I would cry myself to sleep, only to wake up feeling embarrassed and ashamed of the mess I had become. I found it hard to leave social gatherings even when I was sober because I was trying to avoid the inevitable emptiness of my home life. I also had that fear of missing out on the idea that if I went home, if I left too soon, I would miss out on something fun or a life-changing encounter.

With a constant empty feeling inside, you focus on things you can't control, like chance encounters. I felt as though I had to improve my social life, so I worked hard to keep myself busy. But whenever I had more than one invite on the same day, I would be upset that I would have to miss out on something fun because I knew that the next weekend, I would have nothing to do.

It took me too long to realise that the way I was living my life was only making me feel worse. I put so much weight and expectation on every night out, every get-together or event, that they very rarely lived up to it. I was always wishing or hoping for romance or some spontaneous adventure to happen. I would always end up disappointed that this magical chance encounter (the one that would miraculously solve my problems) didn't happen. I would then put all my hopes into the next one. It was a never-ending cycle. What I really needed was to take a break to work on myself. Spending time with friends should have been reward enough, and if I truly craved adventure or passion, it was up to me to go out and find it.

I was not in the right place mentally or emotionally, and drinking excessively was not going to help me. The so-called 'Dutch courage' wasn't going to cure my low self-esteem or self-confidence. What I needed to do was to make some much-needed changes to my life.

So that's what I did.

For a few months, I actively tried to stop drinking as regularly, and instead I worked harder on my health and my fitness. I started eating better and exercising more regularly. I started talking to my friends more and being honest with them. When I asked to see them, I let them know that I didn't want to be alone, I needed some company or a distraction. It wasn't just another invite; it was important. I planned further ahead to ensure my calendar had more things for me to look forward to.

I began to break up the routine of weekday drinking with Friday night football, mid-week meals, and cinema trips. On the weekends I tried to do day trips to somewhere of interest, or to at least go for a long walk or get outside and read a book in the park. I cut back on alcohol because it wasn't helping my anxiety. I identified issues with my work life that needed changing, I spoke with my manager and asked for more responsibility, and I started to push myself towards the next promotion. These things helped me to then also focus on my dating life. I faced my issues head-on and I started to make lasting changes that would turn my mood around.

Lessons Learned

- Be conscious of your own behaviour and look out for red flags.

- When things get too much for you, take a step back and breathe. Go outside and get some fresh air; give yourself a break.

- Drinking alcohol will only make your anxiety and depression worse.

- Break up the routine and be active. Prioritise outdoor and healthy activities like taking a walk.

- Be honest with yourself about how you're feeling. Focus on what you can control and accept what you can't.

- Talk to someone about your struggles and ask for support when you need it.

- Ask your friends for support; tell them you need them.

- Having an adventure by yourself is better than not at all. Being single doesn't mean you can't enjoy life. Don't let it hold you back.

Emotional Consequence

I remember a particularly difficult period in my life when I was worn out from overworking and I had also had my feelings hurt from dating. Things just weren't going well.

I was 31 and had come off the back of a good year when I hit a blip. I found myself working maybe 50 to 60 hours a week every week for several months, and my dating life wasn't going well. I felt dejected. I was extremely stressed and emotionally spent.

Over time, all the stress and everything else began to build up. Because I was working such long hours, I struggled to find the time to exercise or to cook and eat healthy meals. I was going to bed tired and stressed, and I was waking up the same way.

Over a few months, I noticed that my temperament had changed. I was way more agitated and on edge. I felt tired and lethargic. My stomach was in knots, wound up from the stress. I was getting headaches and I started having more frequent visits to the bathroom (a bit like IBS). I even went to see a doctor for a check-up, and it takes a lot for me to do that; to admit that I am unwell. While I was there,

I collapsed in the middle of the doctor's surgery reception area, which certainly sped up the waiting time. Despite all of that and explaining to the doctor that I was working so much, I was not advised to take any time off work. But I knew deep down that I needed to.

However, I felt responsible for the work I was doing, and I didn't want to waste my paid leave on being miserable at home. Perhaps I undersold it to the doctor and downplayed the level of stress that I was feeling, and I should not have done that, but the doctor should have pressed me more and realised the impact that the stress was having on my mind and my body.

Fortunately, my team leader at work pulled me aside one day to talk. She had noticed the change in my demeanour. She asked me what was wrong, and she took a genuine concern for my well-being. We don't do that enough at work or anywhere really, but she knew something was up. She told me that I needed to take some time off to get some rest, and she helped me to find the resource to support my workload. I'm glad that she did, but really, I should have taken action sooner, because every day I felt on edge, like I might snap, lash out, and offend someone out of frustration and anger, which only made things worse. I had all this anger building up inside of me that I wasn't dealing with, and it only wanted to force itself up to the surface at the wrong times. I could have offended someone I cared about or even lost my job due to an angry outburst. At least, that is the fear that I had every day. I was afraid that I would break and I would lose something important or make my situation worse.

Thankfully, I dealt with it in time. It wasn't long after that intervention that I took some time off and realised that I had to make a change. I needed to do something to give myself purpose again. I finally found the inspiration to take the sabbatical I had been postponing for a long time, and I certainly didn't regret it. A sabbatical at that point in time was just what I needed. I went to South and Central America for four months. I went to Rio de Janeiro for Carnival, and I celebrated my 32nd birthday on a yacht in the San Blas Islands. It was the type of break and adventure I needed to reconnect with myself and tick off some major bucket-list items at the same time.

If we don't address these things early on, they can build up to the point of an incident; you could end up saying or doing something that you don't mean to. If you're feeling stressed, it's always good to talk about it with someone, whether it is at work, at home, or just in general. If you don't have someone you feel comfortable talking to about these things, a therapist is always a good option. I have many friends who have spoken with a therapist and they can't praise it enough. It's important to have that outlet to lighten the load that you're carrying.

It is also important to deal with your stress, anger, or frustration. You can do that through physical exercise by playing sports or going to the gym, or even just by going for a walk or a run regularly. Exercise is a great form of stress release, and the endorphins will help to boost your mood too.

Alternatively, finding other ways to relax can be just as effective, whether you try meditation, yoga, a massage, or something else; you need to make time for it. And by making time I mean actually carving out time in your day, even if it is for just 15 minutes. Let's also not forget about sex and masturbation. Both are very natural and effective at helping you to relax, relieve stress, and boost your mood. Whether you're a man or a woman, having a healthy sex life is good for you. It is so important to find ways to release that stress and tension and give your body an outlet for that negative energy, whilst also giving your mind a break by focusing on something more rewarding and beneficial.

Take a holiday. Even if it is a staycation (at home), because scheduling some time off from work gives you something to look forward to. It can help to break up the year and lower your stress levels. But make sure it is a real vacation. By that I mean at least a week but preferably longer to give yourself a real break. Allow yourself time to switch off from the grind and disconnect. Find time for yourself and your loved ones, because it is so important for how we feel as individuals and for strengthening our relationships too. Having fun and creating memories together will last a lot longer than any job that you do.

Moreover, for me, the best thing I have ever done in my life was to travel the world. I have taken three or four sabbaticals in my life, and I am only in my mid-30s. I'm not saying that everyone needs to do that, but if it is possible for you, then I can't recommend it enough. After all, we work for about 50 years of our life. That's crazy when you think about it, especially if you are always doing the same thing. So, we deserve to take some time off, even if it is just for a month or two every few years. Think about it: As children, we always had the summer vacations from school, in addition to all the other breaks. But as adults, we are expected to spend eight to 10 hours a day working at least five days a week, every week for 50 years. That's also crazy. You deserve a break. We will all do.

Nowadays, a lot more companies are offering short sabbaticals after a few years of employment. If you're one of the fortunate ones who has an employer like that, I'd say it is worth whatever financial sacrifice you can make, because it is worth more than money, and it doesn't have to be expensive either.

Think about how much you spend on travel to and from work, on meals out or other work-related expenses. There are savings to be made. Cut down on luxuries like alcohol, expensive foods, snacks (even chocolate) for a few months, and you'll be surprised at what a difference it can make to your savings. A short holiday for a week or a weekend is great, but they are very expensive for the amount of time you are away. Taking a prolonged break has a fundamental effect on your mental health because you can actually switch off from the stress of everyday life. Even if you spent a month at home not working, taking walks, visiting friends and family, making time for your hobbies and personal projects, it is a great way to refresh your mind and body and boost your spirit.

In Barcelona it is very common for working adults to take the entire month of August off for their holidays; employers encourage it. It is so hot then that productivity would be low anyway. It is too hard to concentrate in an office when summer is right outside your window. A long break goes a long way.

Even the occasional 'duvet day' can help you during those particularly tough weeks. I believe the concept of the duvet day originated from companies in the U.S. I don't think it is widely used, but it is an intriguing concept. The idea is that you would be permitted a few days a year that you could phone up on the day you want to take off and give no reason or prior warning. The reason for this is that we all have those moments; those days when you wake up full of dread and fear and you really don't have the strength or energy to face the day.

I have done this from time to time; I have called in sick to my employer and taken off a day because my mental health needed a break. I couldn't bear to go into work and deal with the additional pressure and stress that comes with it; it would not have gone well. I am not encouraging you to do this regularly (it wouldn't be fair to your colleagues and could put your job at risk), but on the rare occasion when you really can't deal with things, give yourself a mental health day. Allow yourself a day to take a break, to rest, to breathe, and to think. Compose yourself, exercise, rest, and prepare yourself for the rest of the week ahead.

Another mood changer (for me anyway) is personal grooming. Every time I get a haircut, have a shave, or buy some new clothes, I feel a boost in my mood. I'm not suggesting compulsive shopping, but taking care of yourself can have its benefits.

Whatever your grooming routine might be, it is good to stay on top of it. When you're feeling down and low, you have a tendency to neglect yourself. I know I've ended up looking like a homeless yeti a few times, and that just adds to my negativity and increases my desire to isolate myself away from the world. But when I have a shave and clean myself up, I feel a little better instantly. So, try not to let it slip; it is all part of the positive mindset.

I'm a little self-conscious, so if I'm not taking care of myself, I feel even more self-conscious of my appearance and I start to hide myself, avoiding eye contact and not going out to social events. If I am feeling self-conscious about the way I look when I'm already feeling a little down, I will decline even an invite for a fun activity with friends or from the woman of my dreams. Then I'll regret it and kick myself for letting it happen. I will feel ashamed and find myself wishing I were in a better place (mentally) and not missing out on life.

We need to take care of ourselves more, look after our bodies and our minds, and deal with our emotions. It is the only way we are going to make the most of life.

If you are feeling sad, emotional, or overwhelmed, you need to find it within yourself to face it and deal with it head-on. Don't ignore it and let it build up. Bottling up our feelings does not help. We need to face them, accept them, and process them so we can move forward. When I feel sad, low, or overcome with anxiety, I try to watch a sad movie and have a cry (or listen to some moving music). I'm not great at feeling vulnerable, but if I watch a sad film alone, I'm more likely to let myself feel the emotion and allow myself to cry. I won't fight the emotion; I'll let myself get lost in the story and cry if I feel it.

As a man, crying has this stigma to it, and although we don't want to be breaking down in tears in public regularly, crying is natural. Any man who claims they don't cry either doesn't ever deal with their emotions properly or they don't know how to. Either way, it is not healthy. Crying when you need to is cathartic. It lets out all the bottled-up tension and stress. It allows you to focus on the issue instead of getting worked up or creating misplaced anger and frustration. Our bodies are literally designed to process emotions in this way.

It is no coincidence that men are more likely to commit suicide. It is probably not a coincidence that more men end up in jail either. Not processing our emotions has negative consequences that cannot be avoided forever. You have to deal with it, whether it be depression or anxiety or stress. You can't walk around life feeling sad, angry, frustrated, or agitated in some way without being affected by it. We need to deal with it.

Stress is a huge issue in society today. The way that we live and work has to change. The COVID pandemic of 2020/21 has shown us that. We need more time for ourselves and for our families. We need more exercise, and we especially need to give our mental health more attention. This is very crucial for our peace and happiness.

Lessons Learned

- Ignoring your emotions has consequences.

- Stress can have a negative impact on both your mental and physical health, so don't ignore it.

- It is important to find a healthy work-life balance. Take time off when you need to disconnect and recharge.

- Pay attention to your mood and behaviour, and take action sooner rather than later. Seek help, give yourself a break, and get plenty of rest.

- Consider taking a sabbatical or a long holiday if possible.

- Give yourself an outlet for negative energy. Find ways to destress and relax.

- Allow yourself to cry, even if you're a man. Ignoring your feelings will only make things worse.

- Stay on top of your personal grooming because it can help to lift your mood.

- Take a mental health day if you really need to.

- Speak to a therapist for extra support.

Facing the Challenge

I like to be challenged. I'm not afraid of it; I grew up competing in sports with my friends and my two brothers. I don't back down from things because the odds are stacked against me. In some cases, it motivates me more. But the point is to be realistic with yourself. I learnt early on that dreaming or being overly optimistic can set you up for a let-down. It is not about diminishing your positivity, but managing your expectations versus reality.

I remember having a conversation with a friend a couple of years ago when I was trying to make a change in my life to move abroad. I was trying to convey to her that I understood the road ahead was going to be tough, but that I was ready for it. I was going into the challenge with my eyes wide open. I knew that finding a well-paid, English-speaking job with a good modern company was going to be hard for me to find in Barcelona while I was living in London, but that didn't mean I wasn't going to try. But for her, that came across as a negative mindse. I know that she was only trying to be positive and encouraging, but I felt that she was dismissing my realistic mindset. I don't think that everyone understands the benefit of being realistic. It isn't about being negative or dismissive, it is about understanding the gravity of the situation you are facing and mentally preparing yourself for it.

Someone who is inherently positive might not need to think like this, but in my experience, if I let myself be too positive and optimistic, it hurts all the more if it doesn't work out. So, I learnt not to get carried away with positive affirmations because it's easy to get caught up in the fantasy of it all and to lose focus. I don't think of myself as a negative person, but I am not a naturally positive person either. I just try to be objective. Some things are simply outside of your control, and no matter how hard you try, you can't change that. That's why it is important not to pin all your hopes on something you can't fully control, but to instead focus on what you can control and then hope it works out in your favour. At least then you are prepared for both outcomes and can take solace in knowing that you did all you could do. I try to be positive and optimistic but prepare myself mentally for the possibility of rejection. It's like developing a thick skin.

Consider the profession of acting, for example. You would have to be a little bit crazy or delusional to think that you were going to become a Hollywood star overnight. Because in reality, even the most successful actors often rely on a bit of luck or fortunate timing before they can get their big break, and that's quite often after years of rejections. But if you go into a career like that with an open mind and a strong will and determination, then even if you do not succeed to the level you dreamt of, you can still be happy with the effort you put in. It is about understanding what is in front of you and accepting the challenge in the road ahead, but not being afraid of it. Instead, you are prepared and willing to roll with the punches and to not be too hard on yourself if it doesn't work out quite as planned.

I think there is a clear difference between someone who is feeling negative and someone who is mentally preparing themselves for something. It is down to us to identify the difference. I think if someone is saying "it won't be easy" or "there's a lot of competition," that type of thing sounds more like a description of the situation. Whereas if someone is saying "I've got no chance," or "knowing my luck," those sound more like negative self-reflection, which might indicate how they are feeling. In those moments, I would encourage you to ask, "what makes you say that?" or "how can I help?" Say something that encourages them to open up or shows them that you are there for them.

Something that I think many people are not aware of is that there are a lot of open-ended phrases or clichés that are thrown around without realising the impact they have on people. When someone is struggling with anxiety or depression, it can be really upsetting to hear something that sounds dismissive. The trouble with phrases like "don't worry, it'll work itself out," or "you'll get there in the end," or "keep your chin up," is that when you are struggling with a negative mindset, you can interpret these words as though the person saying them has put no thought into them at all. It can feel frustrating, as though your feelings are being dismissed like they are not valid.

Think of it like this: Imagine you are at work. You're tired and stressed, and you are stuck with a problem you just don't know how to fix. You ask your boss or your most trusted colleagues for help and they say, "you've got this." You are probably going to be a little surprised and disappointed, because your problem still exists and you're no closer to a solution. From your boss's perspective, they might think they are sounding supportive and showing you that they trust you. When you're not stressed or under pressure, it would probably feel good to hear, but because you're feeling mentally exhausted and vulnerable, what you need is more considered advice and support.

This is what it is like to struggle with depression; you are mentally and emotionally drained every single day. You are exhausted and feel unable to help yourself. You don't need encouragement; you need actual support and understanding.

The reality is, most of the time when a friend or loved one sees that you're feeling down but can't understand or relate to what you are going through, they feel lost. It is hard to know what to say to someone who is depressed if you've never experienced anything like it. We're not taught about it in school. Most of our parents and even ourselves weren't even aware of mental health until recently, so none of us have learnt how to deal with it.

As friends and family, we need to learn how to be there for one another when someone is struggling with their mental health. We need to learn to be more observant of when they are struggling and offer them support in the right way. It is difficult to know what to say, but often we don't need to say anything. We just need to let them know that they are not alone. That their friends and family are there for them. That they are willing to listen to how they feel and acknowledge those feelings without judgement.

Sometimes, we just need to be able to vent our feelings; to let that hurt out. Often, we don't need advice. We just need to know that if we need your help, you will do your best or will assist us in finding someone else who can.

As someone who often struggles with his mental health, I can say that we all need to learn to manage our expectations and prepare ourselves better for some of life's setbacks, because there will be many. Life isn't easy, and things don't always go as planned. But that doesn't mean that we can't be happy or that we should lose hope and give up immediately. Being patient, being resilient, and learning to adapt from time to time is how we are going to survive and even thrive in this life. There will be obstacles and barriers in our way, but if we anticipate them a little more, we can handle them a little better, and together we can find our way past them and keep moving forward.

There is a quote that I find really meaningful from the movie *Rocky Balboa*. If you haven't seen it, I recommend it. There is a moment in the film when Sylvester Stallone (as Rocky) is talking to his son about how hard life is, and he passes on these perfect words of wisdom: "It ain't about how hard ya hit. It's about how hard ya can get hit and keep moving forward. How much ya can take and keep moving forward." We are all stronger than we give ourselves credit for. Human beings are resilient creatures, and life is worth the struggles we must endure. Don't give up. You are not alone; keep moving forward.

Lessons Learned

- Match your expectations to reality. Prepare yourself mentally for the challenges ahead.

- Focus on what you can control and make sure you can be happy and proud of the effort you put in.

- As friends and family, we need to be more observant of those we love; their moods and their behaviours.

- When someone is struggling with their mental health, try to avoid common phrases and instead show them support and listen without judgement.

- Respect each other's feelings, even if you cannot relate to how someone feels.

- No matter how hard you get hit, keep moving forward.

Signposting

It helps when you have something to aim for. My life is much easier to manage when I know what I am doing and where I am heading, but much of the time, I don't have a plan. It is in these moments of uncertainty, when I don't know what I'm moving towards or what I am working for, that I begin to lose hope and start to question myself. If I am not careful, I can end up feeling a little lost, and the self-doubt and negativity will begin to creep in.

This is why it is always good to have something planned for the future, whether short term, long term, or temporary. Having these markers throughout the year can help you to focus and break down your future into smaller chunks rather than being overcome with anxiety about the rest of your life.

Instead, when you think of the future, you think about a shorter and more manageable amount of time that isn't so overwhelming. Work and education are the two simplest and obvious milestones that you can focus on, as typically you can assign an estimated time period to your general progression. This includes each year of study, the length of the course, exams, graduation, as well as work promotions, increased responsibility, and achieving progress goals within your role. For example, when you focus on the current semester of study rather than the entire length of the course, it's easier to achieve that milestone, and you can see real evidence of progress.

The clear benefit of these core areas is the amount of control you can have over them, i.e., the more effort you put in, the more you study and practice, the more likely you are to keep progressing. For example, in my work, I started at the age of 22 at the bottom of the ladder; entry-level. I set myself a goal of earning a promotion every 12 to 18 months at those lower levels. I learnt what the average progression rate was from my colleagues. I learnt what the job description was for the next level so I could focus on what skills I needed to develop. I had a realistic timeline; I had a blueprint of what was required of me, and I had the motivation and the ability to build up those skills. I was then able to tell my manager and my team of my desire to learn and progress so that I could gain the relevant experience to do so. I more or less achieved those goals. It did not go according to plan because of the financial crisis and other factors outside of my control, but I persisted and did all that I could do to ensure I continued to progress, and I did.

Personal relationships, however, are a little less predictable and harder to control. When I was young, I thought I would be married by the time I was 30. As it turns out, that was a little misguided, and my young naive self could not understand the little amount of control I could have over such a target. When it comes to relationships, you can only control what you put into them. You have control over whether or not you ask someone out on a date. You have control over how much attention you give them, how romantic you are, and how much of your life you share with them. You can control how you treat them and how you act around them, but you cannot control how they feel about you.

So, although there are obvious markers like the first date, first kiss, first time you have sex, meeting their friends, and moving in together, you can't fully control them. But you can communicate how you feel to your partner and talk about what you both want from your relationship to ensure you're on the same wavelength. You can then set some goals together that might include buying a house and getting married. Alternatively. you can identify early on if your goals are not compatible and save yourself some future heartbreak.

If you're still searching for your life partner, you need to focus on the progress you are making. If a relationship doesn't work out, you will at least have learnt that you were not right for each other and can rule them out. You might also learn something like what you don't want from a partner, or an area of self-improvement. But be proud that you are putting yourself out there and making an effort. It is important to set achievable goals, like how often you put yourself out there.

If you are single, you could commit to asking out at least three or four people within a certain amount of time or going speed dating. These are the type of goals that you can commit to and achieve without too much stress or anxiety. You can see visible progress as you work towards your monthly or yearly goal. Each marker you pass reassures you that you're making progress, and it encourages and motivates you to keep pushing yourself forward. Retrospectively, they help to remind and reassure you (if you already had one date then you can do it again). Every little marker you pass is proof that you are moving forward; you are heading in the right direction. So even if you feel a little lost, you can remind yourself of the changes you are making to your life and the plans you have in place for the near future.

What about a bucket list? Do you have one? A bucket list is a list of things that you absolutely need to do before you die to make the most of your life. It is a primal urge to live life to the fullest. It is a source of motivation and focus. What will you regret not having done when you look back on your life? A list of things to do before you die may apply some pressure, but it is good pressure. Sometimes we need a kick up the bum; additional motivation to enjoy the here and the now. As human beings, we are susceptible to resigning ourselves to only that what we know; what we are familiar with. It is safer to stay in the nest, and we sometimes forget that the risk of leaping out of it is worth the reward of freedom. Goals like these are just that; a reward—something you have always wanted and dreamt of; something that you cannot allow yourself to pass up. Having a bucket list is a way of telling yourself that this is something you must do no matter what. That is tangible motivation. It really is a royal kick up the arse. And a good one.

You can fill your list with anything. Mine had a few adventurous activities like doing a skydive, a bungee jump, going white water rafting, and scuba diving. They were all achievable, daring, and memorable, and they definitely took me out of my comfort zone. I did them all, and they were some of the most incredible things I have ever done! I have no regrets, no matter how scared I was standing at the edge of that bridge in New Zealand failing to smile convincingly at all my new friends. I look back at that picture of me looking terrified and I laugh, and importantly, I feel nothing but pride and happiness. Why? Because I was so scared beyond belief and I still did it. I loved it. I'd do it again. It was so freeing and exhilarating. One of the best moments of my life.

You don't have to be quite as adventurous, but I would encourage you to challenge yourself and include experiences that take you out of your comfort zone and test you. There should also be big things on there though—let's face it, a list of things to do before you die is a pretty serious list. You should include more ambitious milestones like buying your own home, running a marathon, or achieving long-term professional goals; things that are really important to you. For me this includes things like living abroad, learning a new language, and writing a book; two of which I am doing right now. The other admittedly needs a little work and more focus. I've never written these things down; I don't have a physical list, but I don't need to write them down because they are important to me. I always think about them and I have no doubt I will do them all. Why? Because I won't allow myself not to do them. After all, I can't die until I do. A little dramatic I know, but the point is, they are goals that motivate me, and they keep me focused. They keep me moving forward.

Obviously, your list can change over time. It should. As you get older, you'll begin to tick things off only to replace them with new goals. The things you like can also change over time, and it's ok to remove something if you no longer want to do it. As long as you can live without ever have done it.

When I was younger, I always wanted to get a tattoo, and then as I got older, I realised that there wasn't anything I wanted badly enough to live with for the rest of my life. So I scratched it off the list, and I'm happy with that decision, but for most things, the only way they'll get scratched off is through my determination.

Granted, it is difficult to do everything, especially when I keep adding more and more countries to the list of places I want to visit, but that just keeps me motivated. I'll keep working hard, no matter how many excuses present themselves to me because, in the end, it's important to me. I have something to aim for, to look forward to, and to work towards. It also keeps me in check. If I allow a couple of years to pass and I've not ticked anything off the list or I haven't come close to it, then I sit down and think about what I need to change or do to make it happen. Life is hard. Trust me, I know. But reminding myself that life can also be beautiful, fun, exciting, and incredible, somehow makes those hard parts more bearable. And being able to remind myself of the goals and dreams I've accomplished so far in my life reassures me that I know what's important in life and I am doing my best to make the most of it.

Aside from the bucket list and the bigger life plans, you can also give yourself smaller targets that will help you to break up the year and lighten the load you are carrying. During some of my most trying years, I always made sure that there were at least a few moments that I could focus on and look forward to. Simple things that would give me joy and some relief from my life that had become so hard to deal with every day. These were less like goals and more like markers (signposts) to focus on or look forward to. Things like a holiday, a party, a hike, or an event of some kind. Having something in the calendar to look forward to gives me something to focus on.

When it feels like everything is going against you and you feel overwhelmed, it is a relief to know that in just a few weeks you will have the chance to get away from it all; to have some fun and to be yourself again. Especially holidays, as these give you genuine time to breathe, recharge, and refocus. It is in these moments that we can take a step back and think about the things in our life we need to change. We can focus on the things that we can control. A vacation can make a big difference, but I know that it can be hard to find the money or the company to commit to time away. But we shouldn't let that stop us, whether we visit friends, family, or just stay at home and take walks and get outside more. A break from work and our routines is what we need to refresh our minds.

Take a vacation on your own. I've done it many times because I realised that when I wait for friends to become available, I often miss out entirely, so I go it alone. And when you need to get away; when your mental health needs a break, then it is especially important to overcome those excuses and do what's best for you.

Travelling on your own can be daunting, but it is so common now for people to do it, and the infrastructure is there to make it easy for you. There are also plenty of group-organised trips and excursions available to choose from. Giving yourself a break and a little adventure can remind you of the beauty of life and of this planet we are fortunate to live on. Holidays are significant signposts that break up your year and give you a break from feeling lost and emotionally drained all the time.

But a word of caution: If your mental health has reached this point, where you are just trying to get through the year and you are giving yourself these little events and occasions to look forward to, helping shed some light in the darkness you are feeling, you need to take notice. This should be a warning to you that things are not going well, and you need to take action. We need to remember that things like these are only temporary moments of relief, and putting too much emphasis on them can often make it hard for them to live up to your expectations, leaving you with a sour feeling. It is crucial that you find a way to take action to address the real problems that you are facing. That is the only way to make a lasting change that you will really feel inside. In the short term, these little markers can help to give you something to look forward to when times are hard, but they will not magically make your problems go away.

When you are struggling and you're convincing yourself that you're going nowhere or that you've not accomplished enough, you need to remind yourself of the progress you have made to date. Think about all the things that you have accomplished however small they may be. It all counts. Remember that you are doing the best you can and that you are trying to grow and to improve. Be proud of the person you are and who you are becoming. We are always growing, learning, and evolving over time. And it is the tough times that make us stronger people.

Lessons Learned

- If you're struggling with your mental health, it helps to break up your future into smaller, more manageable chunks of time.

- Set markers for progress and goals to focus on. Give yourself achievable targets and take the necessary actions to achieve them.

- Make yourself a bucket list and motivate yourself to get the most out of life.

- Be open in relationships and talk about your relationship goals to make sure your futures are aligned.

- Short-term signposts like holidays and social events help to interrupt the difficult times with positive moments, but don't rely solely on them.

- Pay attention to your mindset. If you are always looking ahead for moments of escape, something isn't working, and you need to make a change.

Say Yes to Life

Before I went backpacking around Australasia on my own, I was given the best advice possible. Before I left home in England, a colleague of mine said to me that the best advice he could give me was to just "say yes." He said even when you don't feel like going out or doing anything sociable, you should go whenever you get an invite. He said that saying yes had led to some of the best memories he had. It was all about the unexpected adventure and being open to life. I followed his advice, and it resulted in one of the most unexpected and memorable nights of my life; a romantic encounter I had thought was all but lost.

When I arrived in Bangkok as a still fresh-faced 24-year-old, I hadn't had much luck with women. In fact, I hadn't had a romantic encounter of any kind for at least a couple of years, and there wasn't too much to brag about before that. But I had this recurring dream, a fantasy really, that I would meet a beautiful woman and fall in love. I was reluctant to let myself believe it was remotely possible, so I relegated the thought to the confines of my dreams, but a little tickling notion of excitement prevailed. And it didn't take long to become an all-consuming thought. After a disastrous start on my arrival in Bangkok, I woke up full of determination and optimism on the first day. I was adamant that I would make the most of the day, even if I was to be alone.

I headed out in the humid sun to explore what the city had to offer. In addition to embracing the wild cultural differences of crazy traffic, street vendors, and random repetitive music, I had planned to explore the Golden Palace. I had been warned that scammers would try to convince me that, unfortunately, the palace is closed and I should therefore spend my time and money with them, but because I knew better, I politely passed on their 'helpful' advice and continued with my goal for the day. Lo and behold, the palace was open and busy with tourists. After a successful day in the sun seeing all of the sights that I had on my list, I overcame my hesitation and tried the local street vendor food. I felt happy with the small feats I'd achieved for the day, and I returned to my hostel with a smile on my face.

I didn't know what to expect when I first embarked on my solo journey. I had done it before, with a friend, for a shorter duration of time, and so I hoped it would be as similarly fun and adventurous, even on my own. I hoped to meet new people and make new friends, because no matter how confident I am around familiar faces and surroundings, I am inherently shy and reserved. It was a little apprehensive and unsure of whether I would find the confidence within myself to speak to strangers; to put myself out there, outside of my comfort zone. And of course, inevitably, there were moments where that was true. I failed on a few occasions to muster the courage needed to break the ice and introduce myself, but the beauty of long-term travel was that I would have many chances to push myself, and plenty of reasons to do so.

When I returned to my hostel, I had a quick refreshing shower. I then went down to the communal area and forced myself to sit near a few friendly faces in the middle of a conversation. Without hesitation they invited me to join them, and I was instantly rewarded for my efforts. Not long after, a group of girls who were new to the hostel came and joined us. Immediately, one of them caught my eye, my breath, and my heartbeat. I tried not to focus on it and to just enjoy the moment. It was a nice evening, chilled and relaxed. The girls didn't stay long, as they were tired from the journey, but one of them left a lasting impression on me.

The next day, after another productive day full of cultural exploration, I found myself chatting with some of the guys from the evening before. But my mind kept drifting to the girl who stole my heartbeat. Would I see her again? Would we spend any time together? And then, there she was with her friends. She said hello and extended me an invite to join them, but I felt inclined to decline because I hadn't packed the attire to match their glamour. I broke my rule of 'just say yes,' but I genuinely believed I could not meet the required dress code, and so my mood dropped. Had I just lost the opportunity to make a real connection with someone?

Fortunately, I was not alone, and there was no time for self-pity. One of my new friends invited us all to an opening party of a new bar in town. So, at the second opportunity, I embraced the rule of 'yes' once more. After a short time, myself and a friend decided to leave. My mind continued to drift throughout the evening, and then chance intervened. It felt serendipitous because the taxi driver dropped us off in the wrong location, and on our walk home, we happened to stumble upon the English girl who made my nerves tingle with excitement. We spent an unforgettable night together on a rooftop in Bangkok; a moment that renewed my belief in the possibility of love. A moment that would never have existed if I had let my insecurities prevail. It took just a couple of small moments outside of my comfort zone to provide my heart with the kind of passion and excitement it had always longed for.

The romance continued for a while after, helping to shape my travels and to make it an adventure I'd never forget. Meeting her then, in that way, was just what I needed to lift my spirits and to give me hope once again.

Unfortunately, although it started like a fairy tale, we did not find our way to the happy ever after. But I did learn some important lessons. At the time I was not fully comfortable with being vulnerable with another person. I was not ready to be open and honest about my feelings. I was not yet ready to let someone in; not in the way that is needed for love to blossom. I had felt the flicker of love in my heart, but I unconsciously kept her love at bay. The timing for the two of us wasn't right.

I got my heart broken, but it took a while to understand why and to appreciate that it wasn't meant to be. But the experience helped me to grow no end, and it gave me hope and encouragement for the future. I had taken on this adventure on my own, having never lived away from home and having spent many of my previous years struggling with depression. But I found pride in my courage to pursue my dreams, even though it meant going it alone. I had the courage to put myself out there time and again, the courage to be outside of my comfort zone every day, the courage to find love and romance, the courage to face fears and to push myself. I embraced the rule of 'saying yes' and fought the urge to be defensive; to say no or to say nothing.

Another prime example was my move to Barcelona. When I was applying for jobs abroad, I applied to positions in Paris, Amsterdam, Stockholm, Munich, Madrid, Lisbon, and Barcelona. My goal was to secure a job before moving because it was less of a risk, as I did not have a huge amount of savings to fall back on. When I was offered the job in Barcelona, I was excited by the prospect of living there, but I was also apprehensive about the job itself. I was not convinced that it was a good company to work for, but it was my only job offer at the time. I could have chosen not to take it and wait for a better opportunity, but I wasn't convinced that I would find another offer in Barcelona, so I told myself I had to say yes. Even if the job didn't work out, I would be able to fulfil my dream of living abroad, and I would get to do that in Barcelona! Despite my reservations and my fears, I decided to embrace life and seize the opportunity, and I am glad I did.

By saying yes to life, I've gained experiences I would have otherwise missed out on. I've made memorable connections that I'll never forget, and I've made lifelong friends I would never have met had I not said yes. I found more self-confidence and assurance from expanding my life experiences. I have gained so much from these experiences and from learning to say yes more. The lesson was not just to say yes, but to be more open to possibilities. Often, we push life away without realising it because it isn't convenient and we haven't had time to consider it more. We feel tired, we have responsibilities, or we come up with a whole host of reasons (or excuses).

In our everyday lives, we don't notice this because it is drowned out by the routine and formality of work and life. But we can all embrace life a little more. We can be more open to a world of possibilities. We can leave the safety net of our comfort zone and put ourselves out there into the world beyond the normal routine.

Lessons Learned

- Say yes to life. Before you respond to an invite, encourage yourself to be spontaneous. Challenge yourself to say yes.

- Force yourself out of your comfort zone and seize more opportunities, even if they are not perfect. You might gain some worthwhile and memorable experiences.

- Enjoy all the small accomplishments in life.

- When things don't work out how you had hoped, take it as a life lesson.

- Do the things you want to do, even if you have to do it alone. Ask yourself if you can live with never having experienced it.

Mistakes Happen

We all make mistakes. It's a part of being human and growing up. We will often make small mistakes while learning something new because we can't master new skills in an instant. So, we learn to accept our mistakes. You can't change the past. Pay attention to yourself and learn to identify when you've made a mistake. Allow yourself to understand why it is a mistake and how it happened so you can learn how to correct it or avoid it in the future. When we are in the process of learning, we gain a lot of knowledge from experiencing those mistakes, and we learn how to avoid making them in the future.

Life itself could be considered as one big lesson, because trust me when I say this, no one has ever mastered it and there is always something new to learn. Every day of our lives we are learning, taking in new information and experiences, expanding our knowledge, and understanding of ourselves, our families, our communities, and the world that we live in.

We need to accept that we will make mistakes along the way; it is inevitable and unavoidable, so it's important to accept that early on. Sometimes those mistakes can be costly, especially when we are under pressure, feeling stressed, or suffering from a poor state of mind. Regardless of whether we are happy and healthy or otherwise, whenever there is the weight of expectation, importance, time constraints, or other factors that cause stress, we are likely to make mistakes eventually.

Working under pressure, dealing with constant scrutiny, and worrying about consequences or the fear of failure all put your mind under immense pressure. None of us can perform perfectly for long whilst dealing with high levels of stress or anxiety. It is too taxing. Our brains are not limitless; they tire, they need rest, and they need sufficient fuel. The more stress and anxiety we are dealing with, the more likely we are to make mistakes.

Much like when you get drunk and wake up with the fear of regret about the night before. Often people say or do things when intoxicated that they regret because they were not of sound body and mind, and so their judgement and their abilities were impaired. Or, when you are tired and you are trying to work, study, or perform a skill of some kind, you may find yourself getting frustrated and angry with yourself because you are making more and more mistakes. We know that making mistakes is natural, so if we're able to make mistakes when we are sober, when we're happy and healthy, then we can't expect anything different when we are not of sound body and mind.

When we are feeling sleep deprived because we are working too hard or because we are juggling too much, we need to accept that our bodies are not getting enough rest and mistakes are almost inevitable. When we are stressed, depressed, or feeling anxious, the same is also true. Living with depression or anxiety is spending each day under immense psychological pressure, and it is unbelievably taxing. Therefore, we will make mistakes: We might say something we don't mean or do something out of character. And as hard as it is to accept that, we have to learn to forgive ourselves and understand why we said or did what we did. Apologise and make amends. Consider it a life lesson and learn how to ensure it does not happen again.

In my experience, when you are feeling stressed, overwhelmed, or depressed, you can often lash out in anger or frustration and say things you don't mean. It could be a cry for help or just a side effect of living in a constant state of high stress and pressure. We can become overwhelmed with our emotions, and our mental health can become a pressure cooker. There is only so much we can contain. Our minds and our bodies have their limits. If we don't find ways to rest and recover, we will keep making mistakes and making our lives worse, not better. We can't keep punishing ourselves for it either; we need to see the bigger picture. If we are always feeling mentally fatigued and emotionally drained, we can't be expected to keep everything together and perform as we would in a normal and healthy state of being. We need to focus on why we need to take responsibility for our own physical and mental well-being.

An important part of becoming an adult is learning to take responsibility for your actions. We can't get away with blaming things on our siblings forever. As children, our parents teach us to be honest, to own up to the things that we've done, and to take responsibility for our actions. As a child, we learn that if we don't take responsibility then we will still get punished. Why? Because we are making our sibling take the fall and be punished for something they have not done. Passing the blame doesn't ever help anyone in the long run; it only avoids some initial embarrassment and awkwardness, but you don't gain anything from it.

We pay people more professionally when they take on additional responsibilities and have extra pressure to deal with. We reward those able to take on that extra level of stress and scrutiny because it is a hard skill to master. But it isn't just our actions or even our words that we need to take responsibility for, it is also ourselves.

If you have ever taken a commercial flight, you would have been exposed to the safety lesson given in case of an emergency. Assuming you've paid attention to it at least once, you might remember that when oxygen masks are deployed, you are expected to fit your own mask before your child's or anybody else's. Why? Because if you lose oxygen and consciousness, you are of no help to anybody. Taking care of yourself first is not selfishness; it is a basic requirement for survival. The healthier your body and mind are, the more helpful you are to those around you too.

We need to take responsibility for how we think and how we feel on the inside. We have to pay attention to how we are feeling; our state of mind and our bodies. If we get physically injured, we rest—we patch ourselves up or we seek professional help. It should be the same for our mental health too. Not just when we are struggling or in a time of need, but constantly. We need to maintain a positive state of mind just like we put in the work to maintain a healthy body. We need to look after our minds and our bodies to maintain a healthy and happy life. Remember, mistakes will happen if we don't take care of ourselves. Rest when you need to, take a break, take a holiday or a duvet day, or ask for help.

Understanding how we tend to think, behave, or react instinctively in different scenarios can help us to face challenges more appropriately and prepare ourselves better. Understanding how we think and feel about things and why that might be allows us to consider how others may be feeling too. We are all human beings; we all make mistakes, and so we can all struggle from time to time too. But being human means that we can learn from those mistakes. We can change, and we can grow. We must learn to forgive ourselves for the mistakes that we've made, let go of the past, learn from them, and move on. We need to give ourselves and each other more space for mistakes, the time to learn from them, and the understanding of our specific situations—it can only help. If we are struggling, we can appreciate that others could be struggling also. We need to work together to help improve everyone's mental well-being. We need to help ourselves so that we can help others.

Lessons Learned

- Mistakes are an inevitable part of being human and a part of our natural learning process (trial and error).

- Mistakes help us to learn what not to do and what isn't working. They allow us to adapt, change, and improve.

- Don't dwell on mistakes or punish yourself for making one. We all do it. Accept what happened and try to learn from it.

- Forgive yourself for past and current mistakes. Let go of that torment, take responsibility, learn from it, and move on.

- Put your health first. Our minds, like our bodies, have their limits. If you feel tired or stressed, get some rest, and ask for help when you need it.

- Treat your mental health like you would your physical well-being. Make it a regular commitment.

- Understand your own strengths and weaknesses so you can identify a bad decision, and be realistic with your expectations of yourself.

Embrace Failure

Time is a powerful thing. I truly believe that I can do almost anything I put my mind to. Not because I am super talented and everything comes easy to me, but because with enough time I can learn to do it, whatever it is, no matter what. You could say that I'm blessed with a natural tenacity, or you can look at the positive side of my natural stubbornness, but one thing is for sure; I never give up. I hate losing and I'm a naturally competitive person. But the important thing to acknowledge is that with time we can do many things. But persistence is key, and you need to embrace failure along the way. It's important to understand that there is not one single successful person in the world who has never failed. If you haven't failed, you have not truly succeeded. Anything worth doing is hard, and the harder it is, the greater the reward will be when you finally get there.

Failing is part of life. It is how we learn to talk, walk, grow, and achieve anything in life. Failure is key to all success. Therefore, I know that even if I fail, I can still succeed. Whatever the barrier. I can overcome it or navigate my way around it, even if it takes me 1,000 attempts, because on the 1001st try I will get there. Why? Because I have had a thousand experiences—a thousand lessons on what not to do—and with every new lesson I have ruled something else out, adapted, and tweaked my efforts, bringing me closer and closer to achieving my goal. Every failure is knowledge gained. My failures empower me; they make me stronger. Every little test I survive emboldens me; it reinforces my will to survive. You need to face every challenge with the understanding that it does not have to be the end. It won't last forever. You can adapt, evolve, change, and come back stronger. No matter how long it takes, you will get there. Just muster up your best Rob Schneider impression: "You can do it!" Because it doesn't matter if you win by an inch or mile; if you get there the first time or the one millionth. Success is success.

Something else that is worth considering is that 'success' is not necessarily associated with money. The financial emphasis we have put on the word success is unnecessary and quite ridiculous. Success does not mean money. It does not mean being cash rich. Success can be whatever you desire it to be. If your goal is to learn a new skill or to complete a physical challenge for example, then success is when you have achieved that goal and you can feel comfortable and confident in your abilities. And failing is going to be a critical element of this journey, so embrace it. Let it motivate you and comfort you in your efforts.

The other crucial thing to remember is that you don't have to do everything alone. This is one of the hardest lessons I've had to learn and accept. I very much take on my own issues as my own problem, mine alone to overcome.

But it doesn't have to be that way. It isn't weak to ask for help; it is the intelligent thing to do. Why struggle when you don't need to? What activity do you do where you specifically isolate yourself and try to make it as hard as possible to complete? We worship team sports, family life, and friendship groups. Why? Because we want to share our life with other people, achieve things together, and create memories together. So why struggle on your own? Our friends and family want to help; they want to be included.

I'm not saying we need to just unload all of our thoughts and feelings on to every individual and overwhelm them, but talking more and opening up can only help. Especially when it comes to issues or challenges that you are struggling with, seeking help is the wise thing to do. Don't put too much pressure on yourself; no one gets anywhere in life completely alone.

We learn from each other, leverage each other's strengths, and compensate for each other's weaknesses. We are stronger together. We rely on other people all the time for many things; that's how society works. We all contribute a little so we can benefit collectively. We're in this together, so let's try, fail, and succeed together.

Winston Churchill said,

"Success isn't final, failure isn't fatal."

We will not stop growing; we are always learning, and failure is an important part of that. Life is a continuous journey without a destination. So, let's embrace all of it, and take the journey together!

Lessons Learned

- There is no success without failure. Learn to embrace it and appreciate the lessons and knowledge gained from failure.

- Be more forgiving of your failures and accept them as part of the journey.

- Money has no relationship to happiness or success.

- Success is personal, not financial. It is down to you to define what success looks like.

- Ask for help and utilise all your resources to achieve your goals. Accepting help is the wise thing to do; nobody gets anywhere in life by themselves, and we all rely on each other for something.

- Remember that some of the biggest cultural and technological advances have come from failure.

Escapism, a Temporary Solution

For a long time during the early days of my depression, I would watch a lot of movies as my way of escaping life. I would get lost in the fantasy of stories, the possibility that my life could one day be like the movies. I could fall in love and be happy. I could get a great opportunity out of nowhere to go off on an adventure and find happiness.

I spent hundreds of pounds on DVDs, back when they were a thing. They helped me to escape for a little while at a time, and they helped me to process my emotions in some ways. I'm a sensitive guy, and I would often cry whilst watching movies, but I cried so much that it clearly wasn't about the films. They were real tears. I needed to process that pain one way or another because it would just eat me up inside if I didn't.

I watched so many films that I began to get lost in the fantasy that I could one day be an actor. I would get discovered by chance, all my dreams would come true, and I would find my place in the world. So, at the age of 21, once

I had enough money saved up, I decided to invest some of it into uncovering the reality of this fantasy of mine. I paid for a weeklong acting course in London. It wasn't cheap, and it wasn't exactly an acclaimed acting school, but it was a sure-fire way of shaking up my life and snapping myself out of a daydream. It was a chance for me to take myself out of my comfort zone and uncover the fact or fiction of my acting dream. Was it really a passion of mine? Did I have any acting ability and was it something worth pursuing, or was it just a coping mechanism?

I went to London by myself, and I stayed in a hotel nearby while I attended the classes. I met some very beautiful women who were all very friendly but intimidating, and I was the only guy, so there was no hiding in the background. Despite the courage it took for me to enrol in the course to begin with, I was still very unsure of myself and quite introverted at the time. I was too scared to properly introduce myself to the girls, and very self-conscious whilst trying to perform the tasks given. It was a challenging week, and I spent most nights eating alone in an empty hotel restaurant. However, I was putting myself out there, and I was pursuing what I thought was my dream at the time.

To be honest, I found the whole experience a little awkward and embarrassing, I mean, I was too insecure for that kind of emotional vulnerability and attention. I was afraid to tell my family or friends what I was even doing; I lied and pretended I was doing something else entirely. But despite that, I received encouraging feedback from the tutor, and I had never done anything like that before, so it was a real test for me at the time. Perhaps it was a little

too much to try and take on at that moment—a bit like jumping in the deep end and learning to swim—but upon reflection, it was a valuable experience.

I felt proud of how I had performed and proud that I was able to take on something so challenging. I went from having a very quiet and isolated life and drowning in misery to acting out scenes from *The English Patient* in front of a camera and some intimidating beauty. And what is more is that I discovered the truth behind my fantasy: Acting wasn't for me, and it was not a realistic career path for me to consider pursuing any further. This was the underlying truth behind my escape into film. It was just entertainment and a helpful distraction.

If I wanted to find my place in the world, I would have to look elsewhere. It was a relief to be able to rule something out, close the door to that fantasy, and move on. It worked because it motivated me to start looking for other potential career paths and it snapped me back into reality. No more daydreaming about being the next Jason Statham. Instead, I could try out a more realistic career like accountancy. And I did. I enrolled in a course and took on a placement, but this time it took me about two to three weeks to realise that this wasn't for me either. But I was making progress. It was slow, but I was starting to rule things out until I could find a path that worked.

Escapism can work in the short term, distracting you from life's real problems for a moment. But it is not a cure to any pain or issues that you are facing; it is not a solution. Switching off from a hard day's work or giving yourself a break to recover every so often is the best form of escapism, but trying to hide from your reality is not healthy. I may

have gone to drastic lengths to wake myself up from a daydream, but it worked. Taking myself out of my comfort zone and challenging my reality helped me to eventually find a realistic path.

In the end, I tried a few different professions until I found a career of interest that I could genuinely grow and progress in. I also stopped wasting so much money on filling up my cupboard space with films that I had seen dozens of times. The lesson I learnt was that if I really want to know whether I genuinely like something or not, I need to try it, whatever it is. I needed to test myself a little more; push myself to try new things and to get out of my room and into the real world.

I couldn't hide from my problems anymore. I needed to face the world and embrace the challenges ahead, because I am making progress. Even if it isn't always obvious, I am moving forward and not hiding away.

Lessons Learned

- Learn what is a helpful coping mechanism and what is not.

- Pursue your dreams to discover your true passions.

- Trying new things is a great way to learn more about yourself.

- Step out from the protection of your own home and try something new. Sometimes you have to try a lot of different things to find which one is really for you.

- Expand your horizons and embrace a world full of opportunity.

- Escapism is only a short-term solution.

Defence Mechanisms

Self-deprecating humour can be a positive trait for someone to have because it can show modesty and humility. Being able to laugh at yourself is a strength. Not taking yourself too seriously and being able to see the funny side of things is always a positive; it certainly beats being the opposite. If you can't learn to take yourself less seriously and laugh about things, you'll find yourself getting worked up, offended, or annoyed more often. Even though it can be a positive trait, you do have to be a little conscious of your use of it, because if you find yourself doing it too regularly, it could be a sign of low self-esteem.

There was a period in my mid-20s when I started making self-deprecating jokes. I noticed that I wasn't always as comfortable being on the receiving end of a joke as I was making them, even though they were in jest and good-natured. It was an area I felt I needed to work on; a side of my personality or self-confidence I needed to work on. And it did help. I eventually became much more comfortable with it, but that mostly came from working on myself and my mental health. But at times I found myself making more jokes in the opposite manner.

I was struggling with my self-confidence and self-assurance, and I started to project the opposite. I didn't want people to know that I was struggling. I began making sarcastic comments and jokes that were meant to be self-deprecating to show that I was comfortable joking about my appearance or my personality, but really, I was seeking some reassurance. I was hoping for a compliment or a comment of support or reinforcement to help make me feel better about myself.

Instead, I would be left wondering what people thought of me and what I thought about myself. But instead of anyone realising that I was feeling insecure, they thought I was being egotistical or vain. They had no idea that I was actually seeking validation. It wasn't until I became closer friends with people and we talked more openly about things that I learnt how I was coming across. They helped me to identify the jokes as a façade and a negative trait. I realised that I was doing it so often because there was a problem with how I was feeling. I was low on self-confidence and self-esteem, and I needed to work on myself.

I know now that validation does not come from other people, it comes from within. I didn't know this at the time, but I was putting on a brave face. I was trying to convince people that I was happy, confident, and comfortable in my own skin. But really, the truth behind the smile was that I was just trying to hide the pain. Fake it until you make it. But don't do that, because it is terrible advice. You can't fake it. You can't just paper over the cracks and pretend to be something you're not in the hope that you will one day spontaneously morph into it. That is about as realistic as Pinocchio wishing to be a real boy. You can only be as real as you feel.

Another sign that something might be wrong is if you find yourself always responding with short and sharp responses to people, for example, if you say "I'm fine" a lot or you say "no" all the time. Saying you're fine is another way to deflect attention; to avoid any follow-up questions or deter further interest in your life. When you do this too regularly, it is a sign that you're not talking about your problems and you're not dealing with your emotions.

We do this a lot when we struggle with depression or anxiety because we dread the thought of going into detail about how much we are struggling. The attention scares us; it makes us feel vulnerable or weak. But the irony is that by not talking about it, we are making ourselves more vulnerable because we aren't dealing with it.

The same goes for saying "no" a lot. This is a sign that you are closed off to life and that you might be in a negative mindset. If you're saying no to social invitations and spending a lot of time alone, you're probably using it as a way of protecting yourself. You're hiding yourself away.

If you find yourself using defence mechanisms like putting on a brave face, forcing a smile, avoiding questions, or trying to deflect attention away with humour, you should consider those actions as potential red flags to alert you to the possibility that you are not ok; that you are not feeling fully comfortable within yourself. It isn't something to panic about. Identifying these things is a positive. Identifying the use of defence mechanisms and realising that you need to work on yourself is the start of a positive journey.

Making the conscious effort to understand yourself and to work on building a more positive and healthier mindset should be a moment of pride and encouragement.

It takes strength to be able to admit your flaws and to work on yourself; to be someone who can laugh at themselves naturally takes being comfortable in your own skin. You need to reach a point where you are proud of your strengths and fully accept your weaknesses. It will take time to reach that point, but it is possible. Identifying your use and dependency on these defence mechanisms is a key step in changing your behaviour for the better.

Lessons Learned

- Validation doesn't come from other people, it comes from within.

- Saying things like "you're fine" regularly when you're not, faking a smile, or overusing self-deprecating humour to divert attention could all be red flags.

- Pay attention to your own behaviour. Are you using defence mechanisms to hide your issues?

- Take the time to understand your own behaviour and ask yourself why you're doing it. Is there an issue you need to address?

- Talk about your feelings with friends and process your emotions. Don't pretend everything is ok when it's not.

- Be proud of your strengths and learn to accept your weaknesses.

- Take the time to work on yourself.

Social Anxiety

Social anxiety is something that I have experienced regularly throughout my adult life. Being a naturally shy person, I always experience some level of anxiety the first time I interact with new people, whether one on one, in a crowd, or as part of a group. It can vary a lot; sometimes I won't notice it, whereas other times it can be very mild and easily overcome. In other moments, I might freeze or be unable to speak. My throat will go dry and I'll get panic sweats.

The moments leading up to something is the worst part because the anticipation of it can cause me to be so stressed out with worry that it puts my stomach in knots. That then upsets my body and sends me to the bathroom more frequently, which in turn gives me something else to worry about, making me feel even worse. For me, having someone I know there with me to support me, someone to break the ice for me, can relieve a lot of the pressure very quickly. There have been many occasions in my life when I could really have benefited from having that support with me because my social anxiety got the better of me and prevented me from saying or doing something I wanted to do.

For a while, I was too embarrassed to ask questions, and I would pretend that I had heard and understood something even if I hadn't. In hindsight, it would always turn out to be worse for me than the fear of embarrassment of asking the question in the first place. To be honest, that was a lesson I had to learn early on in my professional career. Not asking questions was making me look disengaged or uninterested in my work. If I misunderstood something, it would reduce the accuracy of my work, and my colleagues would then start to doubt my reliability. The reality was that I was very enthusiastic and keen to work hard and progress, but I was shy and scared to speak up at times. When someone finally took the time to be honest with me and explain how I was being perceived by others, it was much easier for me to break through that barrier of insecurity and to start asking questions.

It was the advice I needed to show my true professional personality. I am a naturally curious person, and when I am engaged in something, I want to know everything about it. I started asking more and more questions, and my career progressed much more quickly because I made this change. Sometimes we just need a little help to see the bigger picture and put things into perspective. I needed that feedback to identify a flaw that I needed to change. Asking questions and communicating is a part of being human. It is a key part of how we learn and how we grow, and social anxiety can get in the way of that.

I have been that awkward person in a sociable environment who doesn't feel at all comfortable being there, unsure of himself, not knowing whether I belong there or not. Occasionally, someone would notice and be kind enough to help me out by introducing themselves or inviting me into a conversation or activity. We need to do more of this; be more aware of others, because people are struggling around us all the time in different ways. Often it takes little effort from us to have a positive and meaningful impact on another person.

For example, when I moved to Spain, I didn't really know anyone, so I needed to make new friends. Unlike the English culture, it was much less common to socialise with colleagues from work, and making friends with the locals was not so easy as an expat in Barcelona. I needed to make a conscious effort to put myself out there and to take myself out of my comfort zone regularly to meet more people. I set myself the goal of attending some 'MeetUp' events, eventually pushing myself to go at least once a week. However, it wasn't easy for me. Some days I made excuses; I just didn't feel in the right mood to go or I was feeling too tired to go (the usual excuses). Other days, I did go, but only physically, not mentally.

I remember walking into a language exchange on a couple of different occasions. I had arrived a little late and people had already grouped off into different conversations. I felt too intimidated to interrupt or introduce myself to anyone. Even though everyone was there for the same reason and most of the people tended to be polite and friendly; I still couldn't bring myself to do it. So, instead, I would buy myself a drink and tell myself if I stand in an accessible place with open body language that would be enough. After one drink, I would convince myself that I had put in enough effort; I had tried, so I could now leave with my head held high. Instead, I would go home feeling that I had let myself down, only to realise later that I had made progress. It may not have been what I had hoped for, but I did leave the safety of my comfort zone at least. But the next time I knew that I would have to push myself that little bit more to introduce myself to someone.

I tried to focus on the positive side; I had made an effort once before, so I could definitely do it again. It didn't take more than a couple of visits before I was regularly interacting with others, and I eventually made some genuine connections. If I had not pushed myself and had let the excuses win, I would have been stuck at home wishing I'd had the confidence to go out. You can't make many friends without leaving your house. You can't achieve much without pushing yourself and expanding your boundaries. Setting goals and targets are important steps to take to allow ourselves the freedom we crave. Social anxiety is a real thing, but we don't have to let it overtake our lives and prevent us from being happy; we just need to work on it regularly. Set yourself targets, motivate yourself, ask friends for support, and keep trying. It gets easier the more you do it, because it becomes more familiar and less intimidating.

I can't even count the number of times when I have failed to speak when I've had an involuntary moment of silence. Even when someone offered me a friendly crack in the metaphorical ice barrier, I still failed to break through it; I remained frozen with anxiety. If we are not careful, our anxiety can create a constant disillusion of barriers that keep those moments of human connection as a visible prison of fading moments. Even when a friendly stranger offers me the warmest of hellos, I can still fail to find the words to reply warmly. I have spent so much time caught up in my own head that many of those moments I craved ultimately passed me by. In turn, I would then remind myself of those moments over and over again, silently punishing myself.

By letting my anxiety win, I leave myself in lonely solitude created by my inability to interact with strangers, keeping up a wall that prevents me from expanding my social life with new friendships or romantic encounters. My social anxiety has held me back a lot in life, especially during my 20s, and I still experience it today (albeit less frequently). In many cases, even when I was able to speak, I was so uncomfortable that my face would betray me and reveal my internal misery and awkwardness. That would then be received negatively, as my demeanour would show me to be grumpy or uninterested, and the whole interaction would likely be short-lived. But in those rare moments that I have been able to overcome my anxiety, I have rarely suffered some ill effect. Instead, those moments are quite often worth every ounce of mental anguish felt in those brief moments leading up to it. Yet even with this knowledge, they can still happen. Being comfortable speaking to strangers can be a difficult skill to master for some, but it is always worth trying.

Human connection is worth a few seconds of awkward, embarrassing, or uncomfortable little moments if it leads to creating positive memories or relationships that last a lifetime.

This wall of ice (our anxiety) is something that we create in our own minds. It is something we subconsciously erect to protect ourselves; to prevent us from trusting the wrong people, and to save us from embarrassment or pain (mental or physical). It isn't a bad thing, because it means we are cautious; we've learnt not to trust everyone, and we are looking out for ourselves. Especially if we have been hurt by previous relationships, we are more likely to be a little more protective of our feelings, and that's ok.

But if we are not careful and it goes unnoticed, we may be pushing people away without realising it. We need to pay attention to how we behave in social situations and be conscious of our emotional walls. We need to remind ourselves of all the positive moments that we have gained from being friendly and approachable. We need to remember that all of our friends were once strangers. We need to remind ourselves of how important our social life is and remember that we are safe and we have the power to end a relationship whenever it doesn't feel right.

We need to accept that we have anxiety but acknowledge that if we do not do anything about it, we will continue to miss out on life. We need to remind ourselves that this anxiety we feel is a fear that we have created; it is not real. The feelings and scenarios that we are scared of are not a guaranteed outcome, they are just a warning to ourselves that we've been hurt before and we need to be a little cautious. But we can face it little by little.

We can set ourselves small goals like I did in Barcelona by going to social events each week and challenging myself to speak to one person. We need to keep pushing ourselves out of our comfort zones and then acknowledge our efforts and be proud of ourselves. We need to think about the reality of what we just experienced so next time we can reassure ourselves that it isn't so scary, because we've done it before. Slowly we will become more at ease with those situations, make new connections, and start to overcome our anxiety.

And don't forget to ask for help from friends. Tell them that you are struggling and ask them to support you on these occasions. They can help encourage you, giving you that extra 10% of confidence or reassurance that you need to overcome those barriers.

I understand that asking for help can be a difficult thing to do. For a while, I was too scared and embarrassed to admit to my friends that I was feeling lonely or sad. I was too scared to even ask for some company, because I needed to not be alone. Asking for help can be daunting, and we may even consider it weak (but wrongly so) because nobody achieves anything on their own. We all rely on other people in one way or another, and asking for help should be normal, because sometimes it is necessary.

Even being asked for directions in the middle of the street by a complete stranger can be awkward and intimidating. The sudden rush of fear of having to speak to a stranger; suddenly worrying that you won't be able to help them or will get the answer wrong, and then you feel guilty for sending them the wrong way. Having now lived abroad, I have found myself becoming more at ease with things like this. Even though it was more of a challenge because I had to deal with a language barrier too, that extra pressure and awkwardness forced me to be a little more prepared for the unexpected.

In fact, living abroad and even just being friends with more people from different cultures has had a profound impact on my social awkwardness. This is because I have been more regularly presented to behaviours unfamiliar to me than I was as a British man living in England. A Spanish friend I met at work a long time ago was my first regular introduction to it. And then having travelled to South America and now having lived in Spain, I have been exposed to more physical human contact than I ever had in the UK. Latin cultures are much more open to physical contact; they kiss and hug to great each other hello and goodbye, and they touch each other regularly. This was all a culture shock to me at first. It took me a long time to get used to it.

As an Englishman, if a woman touched me (even by accident) I would instinctively react as though they had a romantic interest in me. The hairs would stand up on the back of my neck and thoughts would race through my mind. Touching wasn't or isn't something we typically do regularly in England, but I am much more used to it now.

I have therefore taken myself out of my comfort so much that I can see the benefits of it in my personality. I am much more comfortable with human affection than I ever was before, and I have benefited no end from living abroad, visiting other cultures, and making friends from faraway places. This is something that I cannot encourage anyone enough to do. We don't need to isolate ourselves to our local surroundings.

Expanding our worlds and embracing other cultures is the only way to really make the most of life. Some of my best memories are from the kindness of strangers in foreign countries when I've felt lost, scared, or alone and I didn't speak the local language. I've learnt a lot from the outside world, and I've embraced every moment of it.

Had I not learnt from all my experiences, I would have had many more awkward and difficult moments, like when I was in Thailand on my first solo backpacking trip. That trip turned out to be a crash course in survival as an independent adult. On my journey from the western islands to Phuket, I found myself in an awkward social entanglement that almost left me stranded in the middle of nowhere. After a chaotic hangover-induced tuk-tuk ride, I arrived at the central bus station in the middle of nowhere (surrounded by jungle). There were so many people there; it felt very chaotic. Me being British and inexperienced with other cultures, I still assumed that there would be a clear order and schedule to things. So, when a lady gave me a coloured sticker and told me my bus was leaving at 5 p.m., I believed her. Even though I didn't feel confident in what I was told, I was too scared to question it. So I thought I would distract myself by talking to other travellers, but my social anxiety kept winning and kept me isolated. Whilst I was feeling flustered, a local man approached me and said,

"You come with me!"

There was no hello or explanation, just a simple order, but my social anxiety kicked in. I felt uneasy and confused, and all I could say was "No, my bus is at 5 p.m."

I wanted to ask for some clarity, but instead, my self-defence mechanism took over. Instead, he took my defensive reply as an insult (as distrust), and now I found myself in an even more awkward situation. He told me to remember that I had turned him down. It dawned on me then that I must have misunderstood something.

Eventually, I noticed that fewer and fewer people were still waiting, and it was starting to get dark. I plucked up the courage and went back to ask about my departure time and got nothing but a blank look of confusion. It became apparent that there were no scheduled departures; no drivers in uniform or organised queues. I was no longer in the UK. I overheard someone announce transport to Phuket (it was the last one of the day). So, survival mode kicked in. There was no time for anxiety; I needed to get to my destination.

But then I noticed the man in charge was the guy I had unintentionally offended. So, to avoid any confrontation, I hid at the back of the queue of backpackers and hid my face as I handed over my backpack for storage and then seamlessly slipped off into the back of the truck like a social ninja. I was so awkward and uncomfortable speaking to strangers at the time that I turned simple interactions into awkward confusion.

By the time I reached my destination, I was so emotionally drained that I went straight to bed and missed out on exploring the buzzing night market. I woke up to find out that it was the last night of the market and I had missed my chance to experience it. My internal fears and insecurities almost derailed my entire journey, and I ended up missing out on experiencing a vibrant local market.

Our anxiety is often worse than reality. We become so caught up in our own negativity that we make things worse for ourselves. We need to force ourselves out of our comfort zone and immerse ourselves in other cultures. Surround yourself with new experiences and leave your comfort zone more often. This will help give you the courage to ask questions more often. It will allow you to adapt to things outside of what is familiar more easily; to better prepare yourself for the whole of the world that we live in and not just what we see in our everyday lives.

Lessons Learned

- Social anxiety is a very common thing to experience; it's completely natural.

- If you get nervous before social occasions and often experience physiological symptoms, you may have social anxiety.

- If you have social anxiety, try taking a deep breath before each event and remind yourself of why you're going. Try listening to some music to calm your nerves. Tell a friend how you feel and ask for support.

- Make a conscious commitment to leave your comfort zone more often. Set yourself goals and commit to them.

- Forgive yourself for your failings and be proud of the progress you make. Even a little progress is still progress.

- Don't be afraid to ask questions; think of them as a tool to increase your understanding of the world and to give yourself more control.

- Expose yourself to different cultures and experience how others live. It will help you to become more comfortable with different social environments.

Confidence

Confidence is one of those things that you can't just switch on and off; it's organic, and it comes from within. For me, it is something I have always struggled with. Some days I can be full of confidence and others I'm a self-conscious and insecure mess. But when I am in a good mood and feeling positive, I'm much more likely to find it within myself to be more outgoing.

According to one of those Myers–Briggs personality tests that I took at work, I am considered to be about 49% introvert and 51% extrovert. And although I don't fully agree with the accuracy of these types of tests, I'd say that in this instance it's a pretty fair assessment of my personality. In most instances, I'm naturally shy, but I tend to find more confidence over time as things become more familiar. When it comes to people, it doesn't matter what scenario I'm in, my inert natural reaction is one of shyness. Many of my friends might not realise it now, but if they were to cast their minds back to when they first met me, they might recall how quiet I was. I would say that I have a good sense of humour, mostly sarcasm and dry wit, but it fits perfectly with the typical British banter I grew up with. But, when I'm with strangers or in unfamiliar surroundings, I tend to keep my jokes to myself. If I do make a joke, I say it quietly so only the person nearest to me can hear rather than everyone, because I'm not ready for that level of attention. But with my friends, it's caution to the wind.

Everyone behaves differently depending on the situation they are in, but I have found that in some cases I can force myself to be a little more outgoing than normal. For example, I worked my way up to a managerial position in my job, and as a manager, you are expected to make decisions on behalf of your team. Even though it felt awkward and unnatural at first, I learnt to accept that it was a part of the role, and if I wanted to progress my career, then I would need to learn to take the lead and speak in front of others regularly. Fortunately, the more you do something, the more comfortable and at ease you feel doing it. The same was true for presenting in front of people. When I first had to do it, I was really nervous, rushing to the bathroom every few minutes beforehand, getting a dry mouth, and mumbling my words whilst speaking too quickly as I tried to rush through it.

Now, I can still get a little nervous or uncomfortable, but without all the physical symptoms. It has become a lot easier, and I feel a lot more confident doing it. Practice may not make it perfect, but it certainly helps to reduce the nervousness and gives back a little control.

Human beings are able to adapt and learn new skills; we just need to find the motivation to step outside of what we're used to and to push ourselves that little bit more.

Playing sport is a funny area when it comes to confidence. I consider myself to be naturally athletic, I'm not good at every sport, but I'm rarely the worst, and with a bit of practice I can usually deliver something respectable. Take football, for instance. I'm good at football (ignore the ridiculous comments from my friends mocking me at this point), but I am. And they can't deny it (as much as they'd like to). But despite believing in my own ability, I can still sometimes lack confidence on a given day or in a specific moment during a game when I doubt myself.

For example, I could have just stolen the ball off the opposition and dribbled past two players when my instinct would kick in and tell me to shoot. Now, when I'm feeling confident, I wouldn't even hesitate to take the shot, but on other days a self-conscious thought would jump into my mind and say, "Don't do it." With nagging self-doubt and my teammates around me trying to convince me to pass to them instead, I can end up making the wrong choice or get caught in two minds and lose the ball. If I do pass the ball to a teammate and they lose possession, I will question why I didn't just trust my instincts in the first place.

When it comes to playing sports, a lot of your confidence will come from playing regularly. The more you play, the more self-assured you're going to be. I've reached a point where if I'm not playing regularly enough, I try to take it less seriously to remove some of the pressure I put on myself. I lower my expectations, try to laugh off any mistake, and carry on playing and enjoying myself. Because it doesn't have to be a big deal. Now that might not sound like much, but it took a lot of growing up for me to get a handle on my competitive nature.

I hate losing, and I was a bad loser. I am stubborn; my mum can vouch for that.

But I learnt that sometimes I can be too hard on myself, and I needed to accept that I will make mistakes; it is inevitable. Even professional footballers make mistakes, especially if they haven't played for a while. They play friendlies and warmup games to prepare themselves for the real thing because they know that they're unlikely to be at their best if they are out of practice or out of rhythm. Learning to be more realistic with my expectations was an important part of managing and understanding my confidence levels.

I also realised early on that I love being the underdog. The whole David versus Goliath thing is something I revel in. As long as the unbalance isn't too much to overcome (it has to be plausible). But I love to test myself and task myself with being the person who makes a difference. If I'm playing in the underdog team, the opposition had better be prepared to work for their win, because I'm going to give it absolutely everything and then some. In those moments, it doesn't even feel like confidence; I'm not weighing up any pros and cons, I'm just doing everything I can to win. Having that motivation or that goal can drive me past any insecurity. Seeing the bigger picture and having something else to focus on other than my specific role can help to take the focus away from myself and ease the pressure. It's that no-time-to-waste scenario; excessive thinking is a luxury you can't afford when you or your team are up against the odds. It's all action and instinct.

Familiarity makes a big difference to my levels of confidence, whatever the situation. Whether it's in personal relationships or at work, the more I see people, the more comfortable I become around them, and the more I do something, the better I become at it. Practice really helps. The more you do something, the more normal it becomes, and the less anxious you will be. Even if you never master the skill fully, you'll be more at ease with it.

Another key area that plays a big role in your mental health is your health and fitness. The better you eat and the more you take care of your body, the better your mind will feel in these scenarios. If you're feeling tired or lethargic because you're not eating right, exercising, or getting enough rest, you're going to find it much harder. Additionally, your self-confidence can be tied to the way you look. For instance, I consider myself to be a little vain, not in a superficial way, but I do take pride in my appearance, and so if I'm not comfortable with how I look, my shyness and insecurities will take over. But when I exercise and eat healthy, I feel good on the inside and feel better about how I look on the outside—and therefore am more confident.

Furthermore, I try to be realistic with my expectations and be honest with myself. I know who I am as a person; what my strengths and weaknesses are. If I identify a weakness that I might benefit from overcoming, I task myself with working to improve it as best as I can. For example, being shy, I force myself to get out of my comfort zone more regularly and to speak to strangers. Setting myself goals and challenging myself means I'm always improving; I'm always trying to be better.

Even if it means facing your fears, it isn't just courage and self-belief, it is motivation too. Take my bungee jump, for example. I had always wanted to do one, and while I was backpacking around New Zealand, the opportunity came up to do the bungee jump I had been dreaming of (off the Kawarau bridge just outside of Queenstown). While on the bus heading to the jump, I felt the nerves and the fear kicking in because I knew that I wasn't completely comfortable with heights (especially if I'm standing on the edge). I think it is the fear of not having control; the idea of a loose bit of ground or a strong gust of wind interfering that scares me. So a bungee jump was definitely going to put me face to face with that fear. But it was one of those things knew I would regret it if I didn't do it. It was a dream of mine; a bucket-list item that I had to do.

When they asked who wanted to go first on the bridge, my hand was straight up; partly because I didn't want to wait around and overthink it and partly because it was November, and I was only wearing shorts. When I was standing on the edge of the bridge with a 141-foot drop in front of me, I was physically terrified, and I have the photos to prove it. The organisers asked me to wave to my friends and smile for the camera, but all I could muster was a slow dramatic wave goodbye and a look of sheer horror. I have a video my friends recorded, and you can hear someone say,

"Oh my god he looks terrified; I don't think he is gonna to do it," (embarrassing but a fair assessment at the time).

But I never doubted myself. No matter how scared I was, I had set myself the goal and I was going to do it. It was a dream of mine; a major bucket-list goal, and I knew I would suffer more with the regret of not doing it than I would with the fear of facing it. The only help I needed was a three, two, one countdown because it focused me; it removed the time for fear and initiated action. Without hesitation, I jumped. It was one of the most incredible experiences of my entire life. I would do it again too, and I'd probably still be just as scared. But I gave myself a goal, and the thought of failure was worse than the fear of doing it.

We are all capable of overcoming our fears. We just need to be patient, set ourselves goals, and even accept a little help along the way. It is important not to let the fear win. Don't let it hold you back from enjoying life. We can find the confidence within if we change the way we think about things. Step outside of your normal routine, push yourself, practice, set goals, and find the motivation to push yourself over the edge of fear and beyond.

Lessons Learned

- You can learn to be more outgoing even if you're a natural introvert.

- Be honest with yourself and work on your weak points..

- Be more understanding of yourself, and don't beat yourself up when you feel anxious. Appreciate the effort you're making.

- Be more realistic with your expectations. Give yourself a reality check, focus on what you can control, and let go of everything else.

- Learn when to take things seriously and when to relax and enjoy yourself. Not everything has to be stressful.

- Maintain a healthy diet; it has a direct influence on your mood and energy levels.

- Try counting down from three when you feel scared. It will focus your brain and ready you for action.

Confidence:
The Long Walk

My main issue with confidence becomes most apparent when you look at my love life. It is something that has hindered me to the point of long and lonely barren periods in my life. It is just one of those things. You can look at somebody and assume that because they are attractive, intelligent, successful, or talented, they must naturally exude confidence, but it doesn't work like that. Some days, I can be looking and feeling great, and I still fail to find the confidence to introduce myself to another human being. And then, in other circumstances, it just flows naturally.

Dating can be a bit of an emotional minefield for a lot of people. It is rarely straightforward and simple, and it can cause a lot of anxiety and stress: Overthinking what to say, overanalysing messages, reading body language, and trying to put your best self forward whilst hiding your insecurities and trying to seem confident. There can be a lot to think about, and it can make us feel vulnerable putting ourselves out there at the risk of being hurt by someone. Dating has always been like that for me; a source of anxiety and stress that has led me to many tears. I've always glorified romance, entertaining fantasies of falling in love and living happily ever after. I put too much emphasis on it, and I inadvertently weighed myself down with pressure.

As a man, dating has an additional point of pressure that comes from the perceived responsibility as the initiator. In most scenarios, the man is still expected to make the first move; to be confident and charming. But if you are not a natural extrovert, this can be a genuine source of stress and anxiety.

Trying to find the courage to take the long walk across a crowded room to break the ice of obscurity in front of strangers is daunting in any setting. At times it can be too much. I know that I have often been too overcome with self-consciousness and fear that I have failed to speak a single word, or I've been so nervous before a date that I had panic sweats and IBS. I can feel so anxious that my stomach is in knots, making me self-conscious of my bodily functions. This makes it hard for me to feel comfortable, be fully relaxed with myself, and be present in the moment. It is stressful and it can be a very difficult barrier to overcome. It is especially hard to put the best version of yourself out there if you're struggling with your mental health. It can be intimidating to approach someone whom you find attractive and intriguing if you're not fully comfortable with who you are and you're feeling self-conscious. You tend to overthink the whole scenario, letting the pressure and anxiety take over.

Like anything, speaking to strangers is something we need to practice for us to become more familiar and more comfortable with it. But the biggest thing about dating is making sure that we are ready. Timing is quite often stated as a crucial ingredient to relationships; meeting someone at the right time, when you are both in the same mindset and looking for the same things. But it will also likely coincide with how you feel about yourself at the time.

I spent a long time putting too much emphasis on finding a partner. For some reason, I believed that falling in love was crucial to my happiness. I believed that meeting the right person would fix all my problems and provide me with a happy life full of adventure. I spent the majority of my 20s overthinking every interaction with women, scrutinising their interest in me as well as our compatibility. Instead, I needed to take a step back and realise that I had plenty of time to find someone. But first I needed to learn to love myself before someone could fall in love with me. I should have just enjoyed my single life and learnt to go with the flow a little more. Unsurprisingly, I had my fair share of lonely years, and whenever I got close to someone, I was never fully able to be myself and let down my walls. It wasn't until I turned 30 and I started to work on myself that I gained more self-confidence and started making more meaningful connections.

I feel a lot less stress and anxiety when I date now. I still experience it, but it is much less debilitating than before. Dating in your 30s or older does bring a new set of challenges, as you both tend to be more concerned with long-term compatibility than when you were younger. People tend to be less likely to be open to casual dating in their 30s (it is often seen as a waste of time). But as you get older, I feel that there is a mutual understanding to remove some of the pressure and the stigma we put on the formalities of dating. I've noticed that more mature women are more likely to make their interest in me clear, removing some of the uncertainty felt on my part. But dating at any age always comes with the complications of trying to figure each other out whilst also trying to enjoy the moment and letting the passion happen.

When I was younger, I would go out to bars with friends, and I would spend most of the night doubting whether or not someone was interested in me. Did she smile at me? Should I introduce myself? How would I even do that? What would I say to her? What if she says no?

"She's beautiful, but I'm not good enough for her, she can do better."

Countless thoughts would race through my mind, the woman in question would leave, and I would reason with myself that it probably wouldn't have worked out anyway. I'm just not naturally confident enough to cross the void and break the ice. It takes a surprising amount of courage to leave your friends, cross the room, and meet a stranger without feeling overcome with anxiety. Some people find it easy; it comes more naturally to them and they don't overthink it. Others can be overconfident.

I remember going out with friends one night in my early 20s. A very outgoing and confident friend of mine needed a 'wingman,' and seemingly I was the only other single guy desperate enough to give it a try. So, I joined him on a quest to introduce ourselves to the opposite sex. It wasn't my natural preference, but it took me out of my comfort zone, and it did feel good to give it a try instead of wondering 'what if.' Even though I felt extremely awkward and intimidated trying to speak to an attractive stranger, I was glad I did it. But it just wasn't for me.

I know I'm capable of talking to women and I have a lot to offer, but it doesn't come naturally; it is something I have to make a conscious effort to do. So when the dating apps removed that big roadblock, I suddenly found a way to meet people and to have a more active love life.

Although it was still hard to meet someone compatible, I at least had the opportunity to practice being comfortable in a dating environment. First dates can be a little intimidating. It isn't easy to be yourself and enjoy the moment without feeling a little anxious.

But the more you date the more comfortable you become, and if you don't take yourself out of your comfort zone from time to time, nothing is going to change.

Online dating (dating apps) has changed the way we date; it has offered a new avenue for making connections. On the surface, it should offer a less stressful way of bringing people together because you can do it from the comfort of your own home.

But in recent times, the emphasis has been put back on the man. You have to ensure you have the best and most unique photographs, the most intriguing bio, and the best messages, or you just aren't worth the time. Because of the algorithms set up by the app owners, only the most popular males can enjoy the more natural approach. Everyone else has to live with a lot more rejection than normal, including a lack of matches and a lot of ghosting. It has removed the stomach-wrenching anxious awkwardness of approaching someone in person, but it has also increased the amount of rejection you have to experience. It is a horrible feeling, and it can really deject your efforts, but we need to find a way to accept the format for what is and to not take these things to heart. Finding a balance between using online apps and meeting someone in person is the healthiest approach.

But the only comfort and confidence you will find is when your happiness doesn't rely on finding love.

The expression "love happens when you least expect it" is true simply because when you are happy and comfortable with yourself and your life, you are much more attractive to your prospective partners, and you are more likely to make a move without putting undue pressure on yourself.

To be honest, dating apps are no longer working in the same way. They force you to spend money to increase your visibility and increase your chance of meeting someone. Plus, the sheer volume of competition, coupled with unrealistic expectations, means that getting dates is no longer quite so simple. This means that I, and other people like me, need to find more organic ways to meet people.

After all, most relationships start at school, university, or work environments; places where you have time to get to know each other, and where people can get to see your real personality. Even if you are shy, you have an improved chance of making a genuine connection. That's why I am more inclined to meet new people the organic way by meeting friends of friends, trying new hobbies, or attending social networking events organised online.

In those environments, the focus is on meeting new people rather than dating, so there is much less pressure, and other people are more likely to break the ice for you.

The best advice I can give you when it comes to talking to strangers or introducing yourself to someone you find attractive is to give yourself a countdown. Admittedly I don't do this enough, but it helped me to jump off the bridge for my bungee jump. Take a deep breath and count down from three, and then do it. And remember that no matter how it turns out, the fact that you've done it is something to be proud of, and the more you get used to doing it, the more natural it will become.

The thing I like most about dating in my 30s is not just the honesty and transparency, but also the fact that I am now in a place where I love myself and I know my worth, so I'm not willing to settle or to change myself to suit someone else. I will no longer sacrifice who I am as a person to avoid being alone. It is important to give yourself credit and not to waste your time with someone who doesn't value you as much as you value them. If they are not willing to make an effort for you; to be flexible or understanding, or they demand more from you than you do from them, ask yourself whether it's worth it.

Toxic relationships don't last, and whether you're a man or a woman, your partner should make as much effort to make you happy as you would do for them.

After all, a real relationship is a partnership, and partners share everything. They work together, they support each other, they care for each other, and they build each other up.

Together they are stronger.

Lessons Learned

- It is important to learn to love yourself first before finding someone else to love.

- Put less pressure on dating and the people you date. There is no rush; you have time to slow down and enjoy it.

- Mentally prepare yourself for each social or dating environment beforehand. Prepare yourself for rejection and try not to take it to heart.

- Put yourself out there. The more you experience dating or unfamiliar social engagements, the more comfortable you will feel in them.

- Attend social networking events, take up a new hobby, and be socially active. Meeting people will become easier when it's a regular occurrence in your life.

- Embrace honesty and transparency when dating, and have the big conversations earlier on to avoid disappointment and heartbreak.

- When introducing yourself to strangers, take a deep breath and count down from three.

The Vulnerability of Sex

Sex certainly gets a lot of attention, but not always in the right way. It is a subject we should talk about more in relation to our insecurities and our anxiety.

Women generally seem a little more comfortable talking about sex in detail with their close friends than men are. And I think this is a lesson we (men) need to learn. It is good to talk about sex; not in a teenage, confusing puberty kind of way, but in a grown-up way to talk about the things that make you feel a little uncomfortable, or to ask for advice or support. Sex is a very intimate act that can often create stress and anxiety. It can make us feel self-conscious as we expose our innermost vulnerabilities.

Fortunately, there are plenty of sources where the social taboo for men is less prevalent. I have read plenty of articles online that address all sorts of intimate topics related to sex, and I think it is healthy to educate yourself about it.

Not just the Karma Sutra, but all the pitfalls and the things that can go wrong too. Read stories of other people's sexual experiences and realise that sex isn't always perfect. There may be some embarrassing moments and the occasional concern, but there are most likely many other people out there who have experienced similar situations.

For men, there is an immense amount of pressure related to sex and your ability as a man to satisfy your partner. I am sure there is for women too. But let us also consider this alongside the fact that men are seemingly more likely to struggle with mental health issues and are still faced with the old social pressure of 'being a man.'

The reality is that the pressure can feel very real; not just for men, but for women too. I certainly feel the pressure as a man, and much of is it is generated by myself and my perceived requirements for being a man. Instead of being in the moment and letting things happen more naturally, you can find yourself struggling with stress and anxiety. You can put so much pressure on yourself to satisfy your partner, partly because you want them to feel good, partly because you feel it is your responsibility to deliver positive results (even though there are two of you). You worry that if it isn't good enough, your partner will leave you and never talk to you again.

Sex is important for any intimate relationship, and it isn't always going to be perfect, especially for your first time with a new partner. It can take time to learn what each other likes, and it can take time to be comfortable enough with each other to talk about it.

Talking about sex with your partner is important for all healthy relationships, because let's face it, we all want to feel good, and we want our partners to feel good too.

Understanding what each other wants from your sex life can help you to both feel fulfilled.

Those aren't easy conversations to have early on when you're still dancing around the dating minefield and figuring each other out, but once you feel comfortable enough with each other, it is a good conversation to have.

A bigger conversation is to talk about anything that you are worried about; any doubts or insecurities you have. Because whether you talk about it or not, we are all vulnerable and exposed during sex. Even if you think you are doing a great job of hiding your discomfort or anxiety, it is quite likely that your partner has noticed that something isn't quite right. Having strong communication in a relationship is always going to help, especially when it comes to something as intimate as sex.

I have certainly had moments when I've been with someone I really liked and wanted to have amazing sex with them; wanted them to feel as good as possible. But before we'd even get to that moment, I'd have already piled a heap of pressure on myself. The stress alone would make me feel anxious, and I'd overthink every moment. I'd be kissing her and trying to enjoy it, trying to be confident and sexy, but I'd be panicking in my head, thinking, "What if I am not good enough? What if it doesn't last long? What if I can't give her an orgasm?" All these doubts and fears can end up ruining the whole experience for yourself or both of you. The fact is that we are all different, and there are no guarantees that the two of you will be a perfect match in the bedroom, but that's ok.

We should be able to accept that you can't please everybody all the time. Men shouldn't chastise themselves for having an off night or for feeling stressed or anxious, and nobody should judge or mock men for it. And the same should be true for women. We should all be allowed to talk about it without judgement, especially in a relationship, because we all want to feel safe and comfortable.

I have had sex that has lasted for three hours, and I've had sex for barely 10 seconds. It happens. Sometimes your body lets you down because your head isn't in the right place. Sure, your diet and exercise routine can play a role, especially when it comes to men's testosterone levels as we get older, but our psychological mindset has a huge impact too. If we're feeling stressed or overwhelmed, our sex lives will take a hit; we can lose our sex drive, and our ability to get aroused (to get an erection and sustain it) can also be affected. Putting additional pressure on ourselves and worrying about sex can dampen the mood.

I've often been so caught up in my own head overthinking everything while being with a woman that my body would struggle to focus on the task at hand. And it can be confusing for your partner if in some ways you are showing that you're ready for sex and in other ways you look uncomfortable or just not into it. If you're worrying about climaxing too soon, getting an erection, keeping it up for long enough, whether you're hard enough, big enough, or as a woman you're worrying about how wet you are, how tight you are, or anything else—your partner is going to sense that something is wrong. They might wrongly start to doubt your interest in them, or they might start to feel self-conscious too.

There are plenty of articles out there covering all sex-related concerns, and I'd certainly recommend reading them. And I'd encourage you to talk to your partner about how you're feeling. It is the best way for you both to feel at ease and enjoy being with each other fully.

Sex can be daunting. Being naked with someone can make you feel exposed, not just physically, but mentally too; worrying about all our imperfections and being self-conscious of the natural noises and scents of our bodies. We can prepare ourselves to feel ready for the intimacy of sex by grooming and taking care of our bodies, but we have to learn to accept our flaws and be comfortable in our own skin.

We need to make our partners feel comfortable and let them know that the things they are self-conscious of are not an issue. Tell them what you like about them and reassure them. Talk to each other in bed. Talking during sex was a big uncomfortable shock to me at first. I was so concerned about being naked and concentrating on the act of sex that the idea of talking about what was happening was unsettling. But talking during sex should be encouraged. Dirty talk can work to enhance the mood, but if you want something particular or you don't like how something feels, you should tell your partner, help them, and guide them.

Trust me, you both want each other and yourself to feel good. The best way to learn what each other likes is to talk about it. Your sex life will only improve because of it. And if you feel insecure about a particular part of your body, you'll benefit from opening up about it at some point in your relationship. Allow your partner to show you that they care and that they are the type of person you want to be with.

Sex is an amazing thing, and it is natural. We put a lot of labels on it, and we shouldn't. We shouldn't judge each other so much on the number of sexual partners we've had. As long as we have been safe and consenting adults, it shouldn't be an issue for any gender. And we need to learn that being naked and having sex with someone is a big moment, but it isn't one we should put quite so much pressure on.

After all, we have all felt a little self-conscious or vulnerable when it comes to sex. I know I've had my moments of embarrassment, but I've also had my moments of absolute euphoria. Feeling a little anxious, insecure, or stressed is all normal, and we need to learn to accept it. We need to normalise feeling like a human being during sex and not expect ourselves to be some sort of romantic sex god every time we do it.

Lessons Learned

- Sex doesn't have to be a big deal. Put less pressure and expectation on yourself. Sex doesn't always have to be perfect.

- Talk about sex. Talk about what you both want, what you like, and what you don't like.

- Talk about your insecurities so you can overcome them together.

- Read about sex. There is a lot of professional advice and personal accounts of relatable sex lives available.

- If you're not ready to talk to your partner, talk to your friends about anything that is bothering you or making you uncomfortable.

- If you're a man, accept that sex is not your sole responsibility; it's a tandem act.

Comfort Food

One of the stereotypes I would sometimes fall into is eating too much comfort food. I can't deny that there were at least a few, likely several occasions where I cried and ate ice cream. Not my finest hour, but at the time it seemed like it helped to treat myself with food that I enjoyed.

But more often than not, it would have the opposite effect. It is obviously not great for your health to be eating junk food regularly, and it does start to affect your energy levels and your mood too. This then has an even bigger negative effect, as you start looking for that comfort food again to lift your spirits. Not to mention the damage it would do to my skin, which would directly impact my already tenuous confidence levels.

I think I get it now; it has taken me a while, but the whole 'cheat day' thing makes sense to me now. If you follow a strict workout regime like an athlete or a Hollywood actor, you will be familiar with the phrase, and if not, a quick Instagram scroll will clear it up. But the essence of it makes logical sense. A cheat day is a reward for working hard and adhering to a strict diet and workout schedule.

But for those of us who love our food, I think the simple rule of eating healthy and allowing yourself one treat meal every so often is a good way to go about it (without going overboard obviously). Because if you are burning off those calories in the gym, playing sports, walking, or another way, you will get an endorphin high from treating yourself, and you won't suffer the same negative mental or physical impact later.

Comfort food is appealing, but it is such a destructive cycle to fall into. It is so easy to lose track of what you are eating, and if you're struggling mentally, it really isn't going to help. Even if it tastes good in the moment, it can have a negative affect that last much longer.

Once I realised the link between what I eat and my energy and positivity levels, I realised I had the ability to help improve my situation. I have said before how important exercise is, but your diet is equally important. If you are knocking back the beers regularly and eating high calorie fatty and salty foods, your brain isn't getting the fuel it needs to function.

Think about it; you are starving your brain of the vitamins and nutrients it needs to process your thoughts, to deal with your emotions, and to recharge the batteries after a hard day. When you are dealing with stress, anxiety, depression, or whatever it is, you need strength to keep going; to keep functioning and to get up in the morning. To drag yourself out of bed and into work. To get outside in the fresh air and enjoy some sunlight that does your body and mind so much good.

I try to think of it a high-performance sports car. If you put the wrong fuel in, it won't be going anywhere fast,

so treat your brain like a Formula 1 car and give it the best chance possible to perform at a high standard.

Plus, as hard as it is to choose the healthy salad, stir fry, or other alternatives to the mouth-watering rack of barbecue ribs and greasy burger, it will make those less healthy options so much more enjoyable when you do have them. The less often you have them, the more you will enjoy it when you do. It becomes a genuine treat.

I noticed the more I had bacon, ice cream, or other treats, the less I enjoyed them. Think about something you haven't had in ages; even just a home-cooked meal. When you lived back home you took it for granted, but now, my god do you miss it. It is so damn good.

The less often you have something, the more you relish it when you do. So, you can still enjoy some junk food on a rare occasion, but it will mean more when you do. Perhaps you'll find you start craving something less destructive but just as enjoyable. As long as you remember that you need to exercise to work it off and eat healthy the rest of the time.

If you're no stranger to Instagram, you'll have seen that there are so many amazingly delicious healthy meals out there. We just forget that healthy doesn't mean tasteless. In fact, many healthy meals are delicious, but the ingredients in it are good for you and form a good nutritious balance.

Eating healthy isn't eating boring; it is just a conscious effort to take in a more balanced diet that will fuel your body and mind for your adventures ahead. Many exercise apps these days offer meal plans and recipe ideas, and there are plenty of bloggers out there on social media providing plenty of ideas for healthy meals that you can recreate for yourself easily. They also cater for the less proficient home chefs out there with simple, easy to follow recipes; so no excuses.

It can even be more affordable to eat healthy; a big bag of rice, pasta, quinoa, and other staples are really cost effective, so the benefit of sacking off the greasy or salty alternative is not just for your waistline, your energy levels, or your positive mood, but also for your wallet.

Lessons Learned

- We all love comfort food, but too much of it is self-destructive.

- Cut back on sugar, salt, and fatty foods, and try to avoid overly processed foods too. What you eat is the fuel your body and brain use to function, so make sure it's getting the nutrients it needs to perform.

- Balance is key to a healthy lifestyle and a happy life. Balance comfort food with healthy meals and regular exercise.

- The less often you eat comfort food, the more of an enjoyable treat it will be.

- When debating what to eat, question what you've been eating recently and ask yourself what you'll benefit from more.

- Healthy meals can be really delicious, so expand your recipe book and search online, or ask friends for their best recipes to try.

Self-doubt and Indecision

My depression first started with university, my first really big life decision. I was so overwhelmed by having to decide my future, a decision that I had built up in my head as life-altering, that it was no surprise that the self-doubt and indecisiveness kicked in. I had lost perspective on who I was as a person and what I wanted from life. No particular career stood out to me, and there were thousands I didn't even know existed. I was lost and confused, and I felt compelled to make a decision under pressure. I had succumbed to social pressure and fell headfirst into depression.

It is difficult to make clear decisions when your head is full of worry and stress. You need to take a step back and remove yourself from the situation; give yourself time to breathe and clear your mind. Take time to focus on what you really want, and speak with friends and family in a more supportive and calming environment.

At that time, I wasn't prepared for not having the answers, and I didn't yet know that no right answer exists.

I was so used to the educational construct of process and resolution. Suddenly being presented with a big life decision with no obvious support became overwhelming very quickly. I needed to talk this through over time; to consider my options fully and to understand that it was not a life-or-death decision. I was young, and I had time on my side.

The indecision continued into other aspects of my life, and spending money was certainly one of them. Part of this was because I was brought up to be responsible with my spending and to save money regularly, and another part was my newfound passion for travel. Every big expense was compared to a potential travel adventure. Would this expense limit my travel funds too much? Would I get as much out of it as I would travelling? If I'm spending a couple of hundred pounds, how many days of travel does that equate to? I was essentially comparing the long-term payoff of the product or service to a lifetime of memories. Now, both of those things are pretty reasonable, but it was an additional thought to contemplate, and I started to doubt my ability to make good decisions.

After my experience with university, I was doubting myself regularly, and I began to overthink almost every decision (big or small). I would even find myself in a clothes shop, looking at an item of clothing for 10 to 30 minutes, doubting whether or not I should buy it. Why? Because I would be thinking about whether or not I really needed it. Does it even look good on me? Is it too expensive? Will I find something better somewhere else? I would be going back and forth over this decision in my mind, and sometimes I would give up and force myself to leave, only to return once more after I'd visited every other similar store and clothing option nearby. And even then I would often end up failing to make the purchase. Now, this wasn't every day, for every decision, but it was more common than I realised. I was filled with self-doubt.

I still experience this sometimes today, just to a lesser extent, but the lasting impact of my university experience is certainly one of overthinking. We need to understand that it is ok to be uncertain or to have doubt, and we need not put so much pressure on ourselves, especially when it comes to small decisions. If we are unsure, we can talk about it, take a deep breath, and calm ourselves before making a decision. And consider the reality of it all: Is buying a t-shirt that you thought you liked, only to get it home and realise it doesn't suit you, a long-lasting bad decision, or can you return it and take pride in yourself for trying something new? A bit of external perspective is always helpful. We can get caught up in our own minds too often. Sometimes we need to think it out, talk it through, or think about what someone we admire or respect might do. Ultimately, remember that it is not a failure if it turns out to be a wrong decision; it is a lesson worth learning.

Another key area of my life that self-doubt has affected regularly is my love life. I could give you so many examples of when I failed to tell someone I liked them or missed the opportunity to steal a kiss and seize the day (to be the hero in my own story). One example of how this has affected my life is a fairly recent one. Only a couple of years ago, whilst I was travelling around Latin America, I met a girl. It was one of those moments when I really felt the benefits of travelling solo and taking myself out of my comfort zone.

When I am travelling by myself for a long period of time, I am forced to be more of an extrovert and to put myself out there more regularly; to take small risks and make myself vulnerable. This is something I can easily avoid in my normal life, supported by a million excuses and the safety net of familiar friends, my home, and a familiar routine.

At this point, I was becoming more comfortable with introducing myself to a stranger. Even though I still felt anxiety and a little nagging doubt, I felt more assured that it was the right thing to do.

So, I'm on a bus heading from Costa Rica to Nicaragua. To begin with, I hadn't worked up the courage to say much more than a reciprocating "hello" to the other travellers. At a rest stop, I noticed a girl who was joining the journey. She was very cute and seemed friendly, but when we boarded the minibus, we weren't sat near each other. However, at the next stop while reboarding, I noticed that there was now a free seat next to her (this was my chance). A little voice inside my head told me to go for it, and I did. It still took me a minute to say hello and introduce myself, but once she smiled and said hello back, I began to relax immediately.

Suddenly the fear had slipped away, and the reality of a pleasant conversation sunk in. Isn't it always the same, all this anxiety? You have all this worry and fear, and then you realise it really isn't so bad. We work these situations up in our heads. We get lost in our imagination, controlled by fear, and we make something so simple or innocent out to become this big moment of dread, when in many cases, the reality doesn't match our thoughts.

We had an enjoyable conversation and we exchanged numbers, and that night I got myself an invite to join her and her friends in a local bar. Just like that, the small moment of courage I had to sit in an empty seat next to a pretty girl and say hi, and now I was making new friends.

We ended up spending the next few weeks together as a group of friends. During this time, each day I was thinking about whether or not I should 'make a move' in a romantic sense. But I doubted whether or not she liked me in a romantic way, or whether we had enough in common. I questioned whether it would be fair to her if I was to leave on my travels again soon. I doubted my own intentions.

We enjoyed each other's company, and there were flirty and intimate moments shared that should have reassured me, but my ability to turn a simple decision into a huge life-changing one was expert. Instead of allowing myself to breathe and to be present in the moment, I was overthinking my feelings, our long-term compatibility, what might happen next, and whether someone would get hurt. A whirlwind of doubts and fears took over my mind and interfered with my connection to her. All I needed to do was to tell her that I liked her, and to kiss her when she wanted to be kissed.

I did not need to consider our entire future together or to take sole responsibility for it. What I needed to do was to put less pressure on myself and the situation, to let go of my fears, and to go with the flow. It's good to consider someone else's feelings and to be respectful, but it's not good to put so much pressure on yourself. You are not the only one who makes the decision. But society does put pressure on the man to be the instigator, and that can make us feel responsible for what happens. If this leads to us feeling confused or anxious, we should talk about that with the other person or at least with some friends so we can process our feelings externally. We internalise too much, and that can escalate our anxiety as our fears begin to feed more fears.

After a couple of enjoyable weeks together, we spent the day at a beautiful volcanic lake, and all I could think about was kissing her. In the evening, we sat close together in a beautiful park, and I sensed she wanted me to kiss her. But my anxiety took over, and we ended the night early. I had convinced myself that because I was leaving the next day, it would be wrong for me to lead her on. A week later and we were still talking, and I found myself wishing I had done something. So I decided to change my plans and surprise her for her birthday. But even after that big gesture, I still needed her friend to intervene. Once we were alone, she took over the responsibility and made the first move (thankfully).

We spent the rest of our time together, enjoying our adventure, but we never spoke about it, and my anxiety remained. I still had the same worries; they were just less controlling than they were before. Every day was a battle between my doubts and my desires. I struggled to fully enjoy the moments we spent together; moments that could have been even more memorable and happier.

Allowing yourself to overthink things and to constantly doubt yourself and your decisions impacts your life negatively. You will miss out on happy moments or fail to be present in them. I want to enjoy my life to the fullest and not overthink everything, and that is something

I consciously work on. I forgave myself for my earlier mistakes and started to trust myself again.

I now understand that my tendency to overthink is embedded in my capacity to analyse a situation, to consider all perspectives, and to see the big picture. This helps me no end in a professional environment, but it can at times be a burden, especially in my personal life by causing unnecessary stress (just ask my hairline). I'm learning to separate the two, so when I start to overthink things, I try to take a deep breath and think about whether it's really necessary. I'm more self-aware, so when I'm overthinking, I remind myself that I need to be present in the moment before its gone. If I'm genuinely worried, I try to talk about it so I can get it off my mind and enjoy life instead of worrying about it.

I know now that I don't always have to have the answers, and I don't need to make decisions for other people. It is not my responsibility. I am allowed to make the wrong choice and to learn from it. After all, the only way to learn and to grow is to experience life. Whether the choice you make works out the way you want it to or not, you still took action and embraced life. But to fail to make the decision is a failure to live. Be more in the moment and be more in life.

Lessons Learned

- When self-doubt creeps in, take a moment to breathe, take a walk, and remove yourself from the situation for a moment.

- Ask for help and advice, talk things through with friends or family, and externalise those feelings.

- Put the decision into perspective. Is it really a big deal? Can you change your mind later?

- It's natural and ok to be unsure and to have doubts. Remind yourself of that when it happens.

- You don't need to know all the answers, and you're not solely responsible when decisions affect more than yourself.

- Forgive yourself when you make a mistake and consider it a learning experience.

Imposter Syndrome

Imposter syndrome, that feeling that you don't belong, is more common than we realise. I am sure that this type of feeling can occur in all sorts of situations. I know I have felt it during a few social occasions, but for the most part, I often feel like an imposter in a professional work environment.

Feeling like an imposter is when your inner voice questions your worthiness. It happens to me most when my confidence is particularly low, but given my struggles over the last decade or so, it has been an almost ever-present feeling during my career. Constantly worrying that any task or new responsibility I've been given will prove to be an insurmountable task, and I will ultimately fail and the let the team down. Without reason, I will feel a sense of dread, secretly hoping that they will change their minds, or that someone will step up and take it away from me.

Feeling like an imposter is when you feel like you do not belong, as though you are one mistake away from getting found out. It is ridiculous really, and most likely an irrational fear that is interfering with your ability to perform at the highest level, holding you back from your full potential. Whether it is caused by a fear of failure, a lack of self-belief, or another symptom of depression, it is very real and it can affect any one of us.

It can feel as though you are living a lie, and one day someone will discover that you are not as intelligent as you or others thought. That is no way to live; spending every day worrying that people will realise that you do not deserve your job; that somehow you have been faking it. Fearing that any day you could end up losing your job and consequently struggle to find another.

It's that sinking feeling in your stomach when you want to ask a question, but you worry that by asking it, you will be perceived as unintelligent, and you will be mocked for not knowing the answer. It is that feeling of treading water, just getting by each day, trying not to draw too much attention to yourself. You avoid the big questions, doubt the intentions behind a compliment, and question the authenticity of positive statements made about yourself. You doubt your accomplishments, believing that perhaps you had just gotten lucky, or that they were not as impressive as they could have or should have been if you were really deserving of them.

Whether it is because you are a perfectionist or because you set such high standards and expectations for yourself, it is your thoughts that are creating this feeling of fraud. I am certainly guilty of both of those things, and I developed skills through my career that helped me a lot.

One such skill was learning to ask questions. I learnt this early on whilst trying to progress my career. After pressing my manager for information on what was holding me back, it was suggested that I showed a lack of interest and enthusiasm because I didn't ask questions. I felt like asking a question would make me look stupid, like I didn't understand anything, but my colleagues interpreted my silence as a sign that I wasn't listening or that I didn't care about my work. It is all about perspective.

I learnt to see the art of asking a question as a sign of engagement and intelligence, and this 'reframing' of my own internalisation led to a change in my behaviour. I now understood that although I was worried about something, it didn't necessarily mean it was true. I realised that other people see things differently, and so, instead of worrying, I needed to ask questions to see the bigger picture and to put my thoughts into perspective.

Learning to ask questions and to see things from other people's point of view helps me to accept and appreciate constructive feedback. This in turn then aided me in learning to take criticism and to accept compliments. I still struggle somewhat with the latter, but I allow myself to hear them and appreciate their value, even if I don't know how to react or respond to them. Also, my habit of responding defensively with a polite dismissal or a self-deprecating joke has diminished.

However, with the former, learning to take criticism was something I saw as a positive challenge. I wanted to progress my career, and my ambition outweighed my self-doubt. I once again reframed the idea of criticism to be 'constructive feedback' instead, dismissing anything unhelpful and pushing back to question the root cause because I wanted to understand any flaw or mistake that I was making. I saw it as an opportunity to improve my performance and to take away any excuse for my colleagues to hold me back. It was also a chance to remove any excuse for me to question my own credibility (reducing the opportunity for self-doubt).

Gaining feedback from my colleagues would give me physical evidence of my right to be there whilst also appeasing my own mind that I am not perfect and have areas to work on. It would focus that area of doubt into an opportunity for positive improvements.

Whenever I feel like an imposter now, I try to remind myself of my accomplishments and of the compliments or positive feedback I have received along the way. I remind myself of the areas I have improved in and find self-belief in my ability to continue to improve. Even if I don't feel as though I belong for a moment, I know deep down that I can fill in the gaps where I am missing something and remind myself of my existing strengths in the meantime.

I sometimes also like to consider the performance of my peers. It can be a risky strategy to compare yourself to others, but I have found that in a professional work environment, you rarely come across a perfect employee. Everyone has their strengths and their weaknesses. Seeing that helps me to understand that although I may not be perfect, my colleagues aren't either. I am ok with giving myself higher standards to achieve than others, as long as I remind myself that they are not always going to be achievable, and I need to appreciate the progress I make along the way. I need to remember that I do have strengths and I do belong here as much as everyone else does. Putting those things into perspectives allows me to push myself forward without weighing myself down with unrealistic expectations.

Lessons Learned

- When you feel like an imposter, remember that it is normal to feel that way. It is just your anxiety making you doubt yourself.

- Remind yourself that you have value and that you do belong. Think about the list of things you love about yourself and remind yourself of your strengths.

- Learn to trust your peers more and accept their compliments and positive feedback.

- Remind yourself that your colleagues and friends do not see you in the negative way your anxiety is telling you.

- Appreciate your achievements and acknowledge your progress to date.

- Reframe your thinking. Asking questions doesn't make you sound dumb; it shows you are engaged and willing to learn. Criticism becomes constructive feedback.

- Ask for constructive feedback and see it as an opportunity for growth.

It's Ok to Say No

From the very first moment I started to work for a living, I had an unrivalled commitment and dedication to the job I was employed to do. I always wanted to show that I was hardworking and willing to learn. I wanted to do whatever it took to progress my career; I was young and ambitious, and I wanted to move forward quickly. I was so innocent and naive, I genuinely thought that all it would take is hard work. I thought I would be noticed and commended for my hard work and commitment; my responsibilities would increase, my stature would escalate, and then success would follow. I always felt compelled to do as I was asked and more; I would always try to go above and beyond and to be pro-active.

I didn't like to say no. I didn't feel comfortable with it; I felt as though I always had to say yes. If I was asked to take on a new task or to help out a colleague, I wouldn't hesitate to say yes, even if I was already busy. Even if saying yes meant putting myself at a disadvantage by giving myself too much work to handle.

I would say yes even if I felt unfairly overloaded with work. I would just politely agree and then internalise my anger and frustration. I said yes because as an employee I thought that it was my duty; that I had no real say in the matter. So I would keep taking on more than I could handle, to the point that I would be overloaded with stress.

Dwayne 'The Rock' Johnson is famous for his motto of "always be the hardest worker in the room," but I have to say that this isn't always the best policy. Sometimes it's better to be the smartest worker. By always saying yes, you end up working twice as hard as everybody else, but you are also twice as stressed, and when you're stressed and overworked you make mistakes. Not only that, but your mental and physical health can suffer because of it too.

When I learnt that it was ok to say no, I learnt to look out for myself more. I learnt that it wasn't rude, and it didn't lead to a punishment or dismissal of any kind. If anything, it is respected and understood. When your boss or your colleagues ask for a favour or assistance, it is good to want to help, but if it is going to put you under additional strain, you're entitled to say you don't have the time, capacity, or energy to take on extra work. If you explain to them what you are already working on and what you are responsible for, they will understand. They probably didn't realise how busy you are; maybe they asked you out of preference but didn't understand your workload. When your boss understands that you have too much work to do, it is in their best interest to find a way to unburden you. You'll be more likely to stay working there longer if you're happy, and you'll be more likely to produce better work if you're not struggling to get through each day. So, it's ok to say no, just do it in a polite and constructive way. If they don't support you or continue to take advantage of you, consider finding a new employer and walk away from a toxic work environment. It's ok to say no to stress and suffering. You've got to look out for yourself.

This is also true for relationships, friendships, and families. Some people just can't help but be helpful. Some people are so naturally unselfish, kind, and giving that they forget to look after themselves, always taking on other people's burdens even if they are struggling themselves. It is good to be kind, caring, and helpful, but it is also good to look after your health. If helping someone is putting additional stress or strain on your life or your relationships, it's ok to say no. It's ok to show that you care and that you want to help but that you're not in a position to at this time. Offer to help them to find someone who can help, but don't just sacrifice your own time and energy if you really can't afford to. You are of no help to anyone if you're suffering from poor mental or physical health because you've overextended yourself. You won't be able to help anyone if you burn yourself out.

A burnout is very real; I've been there. I've worked myself into the ground with stress and worry, with excessive hours in the office and strained relationships, my mental and physical health both deteriorated quickly. So don't avoid the conversation. Saying no to the odd request is good but not always enough. Sometimes you need to talk about your roles within a friendship or a relationship of any kind. The people you love don't always know how hard you work and how much effort you put into your relationships with them.

Sometimes you need to tell them and let them know if you feel like you're putting in much more effort than they are.

Ask to share responsibilities. Ask for help with certain things. Explain to them what you do for them and how you're feeling, but be calm and constructive. It's ok to show emotion, but anger and frustration can elicit a negative response, so take a deep breath and count to five to compose yourself if you need to. If you're struggling to manage all of your responsibilities across all the four pillars of your work, home, love, and social life, as well as maintaining your physical health, your loved ones need to know. Do not let frustration lead to resentment. Talk about it. Open a dialogue so that you can find a mutual resolution that benefits you all. No one wants you to struggle, and you don't need to. Remember that it's ok to say no.

Lessons Learned

- It's ok to say no, and sometimes it's necessary.

- It's good to work hard but better to work smart. Make it clear to your manager when you're doing too much and you need more support.

- Put things into perspective and consider whether you are taking on too much. Learn to set boundaries.

- Burnout is a real thing, and it can have a detrimental on your health, so take action before you reach this point.

- Talk to your friends and loved ones and open a dialogue about your relationships. Let them know when you feel taken advantage of or when you need to see more effort and support from them.

- It's good to be helpful, but not to the detriment of your health.

- Ask for help and utilise the resources you have available to you.

Know When to Quit

I am naturally stubborn at times. I have this memory as a child, a silly one really, of me getting all worked up over an innocuous rock, of all things. We were on holiday and on a nature walk when I stumbled across an interesting-looking stone. I tried to dig it out, but the task quickly became much greater than I had anticipated. But I was determined to get it out. I'm not sure how old I was, but it must have been under 10 years old, and at that age, I didn't yet understand my tendency to overcommit. I was stubborn and relentless in my pursuit of things. I was incapable of knowing when to quit. As my parents urged me to move on, I became agitated quickly, infuriated with my struggle to free this random object. My mood rapidly shifted from contentment to anger and disappointment. I hated failure, even if it was for something as random and meaningless as digging up a rock.

As we struggle with our mental health, we tend to focus on different things; issues that might seem small to others become bigger and bigger to us as our inner thoughts take over. When you're in a negative state of mind, the negativity usually wins. We can let our fears and worries take over and assign greater emphasis to things than is required. Whether it is the fear that one small failure will lead to another and another, or the simple desire to pursue a win of any kind, we can get lost in our emotions.

There were times when I would play a video game and I would keep playing for hours and hours until I completed a 'sufficient' amount of it. I couldn't stop playing unless I finished on a high. I would get increasingly frustrated and angry until my mood turned sour and any enjoyment from victory was lost. This feeling affected a lot of things, like feeling resentment of colleagues gaining success or praise that you missed out on, friends breaking plans, or anything that could possibly be deemed as bad news. And although some of the negativity I felt was aimed towards the luck or good fortune of others, those frustrations would turn to disappointment and even anger towards myself and my situation. It was always connected to my high expectations for myself. I didn't know when to quit.

A part of growing up is learning to let go of things. Being able to judge more clearly when you should fully invest yourself or lower your expectations and go in with a more open mind.

When I was younger, it was always all or nothing. I hated losing, and I hated feeling like a failure. As I got older, I learnt to choose my battles better. During my most difficult battles with depression, I was always fighting, against everything and myself; always. It was hard, emotionally draining, and unrewarding. But as I began to improve my mental health and find more acceptance and comfort within myself, I found my more laid-back side. I am still naturally competitive and a little stubborn, but in a more controlled way. I can still have my moments, but I'm able to let go of those and forgive myself for those moments of weakness.

Knowing when to quit and understanding your mood better is easier said than done. When your emotions are taking over it is hard to be rational; it is hard to accept defeat or simply let go.

Before that happens, we need to ask ourselves a question: Is this worth it? How much of my energy should I invest in this? Make a deal with yourself; have a plan. Know beforehand when enough is enough. Set yourself a goal or a cut-off time and stick to it. Set more realistic expectations. If it does not go to plan, does it really matter? Maybe it isn't a video game, a sport, or any form of competition; maybe it is a work project or even a new friendship or relationship of some kind. We often subconsciously apply weight to the meaning of things without realising, and when those envisioned rewards fail to materialise, we feel disappointed or dejected. But if we can learn to take things as they come and be a little more laid back, lower our expectations, and be more open to unexpected possibilities, we will be less disappointed when we couldn't foresee the outcome.

This is the approach I take to a new friendship or to my dating life; to just take each meeting as it comes and have no expectations for the future. I allow myself to be in the moment and to get to know another human being at a natural pace. It helps a lot and puts less pressure on my own behaviour and that of other individuals whose intentions may not align with my own. Talking about it and discussing your expectations together also helps.

That was the change I noticed to dating in my 30s; discussing long-term desires on the first few dates. As we get older and we look to settle down, people tend to be less open to taking life as it comes; we want to know if we should invest our time in someone. We want to know if it's going to waste the time of what we deem to be a biological ticking clock. In their 20s, most people tend not to care so much about long-term compatibility because they're not worried about time. It helps to set out those expectations early on to ensure you are both on the same wavelength. This avoids discovering an unavoidable impasse years into a committed relationship. But we should also remember that although we are older and looking for something more lasting, we are still allowed some moments of fun and spontaneity without worrying about the pressure of compatibility.

It is the same with friendships. We are more selective of who we spend our time with when we're older because we have a better idea of who we are and whose company we value most. It is important to know when you're in a toxic friendship or relationship or when you're not gaining anything positive from it. It can be hard to end a relationship with someone, but sometimes it is the best thing to do for your mental health and well-being. Don't waste your time and energy on someone who doesn't appreciate you or contributes negatively to your mental health.

It is important to know when to quit to save yourself pain in the long run. But we can avoid reaching that point altogether if we anticipate the fallout from doing something competitive. We can prepare ourselves for it better by aiming a little lower with our targets. We can be more realistic with our expectations for whatever scenario we are facing; competition, work, or relationships. We can set realistic goals and benchmarks to aim for and identify when things aren't working out. We can pay attention to how we are feeling and what we are getting from it. If it is negative and not going how we anticipated, we can reassess it. Is it still worth our time and energy or is it no longer of value to us? We need to understand the situation, pay attention to our mood, and consider our tendencies to help us avoid unnecessary and avoidable grief and torment. We can always walk away and give ourselves time to reflect. Even if it is hard to quit, we can take value from the lessons we've learnt from the whole experience.

We need to pay attention to our mental health and identify when these behaviours occur more frequently. Then we can find a better outlet for our negative energy. Remember the role of acceptance: Accept that you struggle with this behaviour so you can do something about it. Remember the role of exercise: It can be a great way to channel that stubbornness and turn it into something more positive. Ease some of that pressure on yourself by setting more realistic expectations. Identify when things aren't going to plan, and allow yourself to quit by seeing the benefit of it. Do what's best for your mental health.

Lessons Learned

- Reframe your thinking: Quitting isn't failure; sometimes it is necessary.

- Know when to quit for the good of your mental health. Don't punish yourself and prolong the suffering.

- Choose your battles. Think about how much energy it is worth investing. Sometimes it is better to walk away.

- Set your expectations early on and be realistic. Set yourself a minimum target and know when to stop.

- Be honest and upfront in relationships and make your goals clear early on to avoid disappointment.

- Remove toxic relationships from your life and surround yourself with positive people.

- Pay attention to your mood, plan ahead, and know when to walk away.

- Remember the rule of acceptance and own your struggles.

- Keep up your exercise and stress relief activities to help maintain balance.

Breaking the Negative Cycle

There was a period during some of my darkest days that my OCD (obsessive-compulsive disorder) began to flare up in new and infuriating ways. I could never understand how some people would find themselves stuck in these repetitive action cycles; but, as I was struggling to deal with my depression and my anxiety, this was an additional issue I found myself contending with. When it was at its worse, I would be leaving a room, and the moment I grabbed hold of the door handle I would hear these negative thoughts in my head, and I couldn't bring myself to just let go and walk out whilst thinking it. It was almost as though if I did let go and complete the action, the negative thought would somehow come true. For example, I'd have this intrusive negative thought that someone I cared about would die, and so if I let go of the handle at that moment, I would somehow have contributed towards it happening in real life. It seems so silly, but when you're consumed with depression, all simple rational thoughts can become indistinguishable.

An 'intrusive thought' is an unwanted thought that is sudden and involuntary, and they can be disturbing and explicit. They can cause shock and distress, and you can feel ashamed for having them, but they are not a reflection of who you are or how you really think or feel. They are caused by your anxiety.

Whenever I had one of these thoughts, I would feel compelled to keep repeating the same motion over and over again out of fear that if I didn't, I would somehow make it come true. I was unconsciously torturing myself, thinking over and over about things that I'd done wrong, mistakes that I'd made, or these disturbing thoughts of death and violence.

I convinced myself that I had to think of something positive before I could stop what I was doing, but positive thoughts were hard to come by; there was so much negativity in my head. It would be increasingly infuriating, making me feel worse and worse as I became more agitated with myself. I felt disturbed by the thoughts that I had, and trying to think 'against' them made me feel worse.

It is deeply upsetting to find yourself struggling to complete such a simple action as using a door handle to leave a room, flicking a light switch on and off, or washing your hands, which I would do so much that my skin would dry out and crack. It was embarrassing to even consider admitting to dealing with what seemed like such a silly flaw; something that others would struggle to relate to. Every time it happened, I judged myself negatively. Even when I tried to shake it off and angrily pull my hand away from the open door, I would instead start closing the door and reopening it to counteract what I'd just done.

Alternatively, I'd find myself clicking the light switch on and off instead like I was just transferring the pain and negative energy from one innocuous action to another. It was a negative cycle that was hard to break. I felt trapped, weak, and ridiculous all at the same time.

Eventually, I began to focus on the fact that the main issue was these negative thoughts, so I tried to insert positive ones to counter the problem. I would bring up positive memories, thoughts of things that I like to do, food I enjoy eating, and other such thoughts. But I would always find myself reverting back to the negativity, and as soon as I moved my hand away, I'd be drawn back into repeating the move again and again. I could just not bring myself to let go and move on. I was always caught thinking that I was failing, that somehow, because I couldn't complete a simple task without thinking negatively, I was less of a person. I judged myself for it, and I think on some level I was punishing myself for that simple and forgivable failing.

But then I began to insert the name and image of a friend or a loved one into my mind instead; someone who has enriched my life. Although I found myself having to say several different names of people in my head, I couldn't deny that they were all positive thoughts, and therefore I was able to complete the action only once. The difference was that the repetitive nature of the OCD was transferred from an action to a thought inside my head. And, because I was thinking of the names of people I care about, the negativity became positivity. It didn't solve things instantly, but over time I gained control of my OCD and repressed the repetitive actions. I built up a solid list of favoured names who would enter my thoughts and help me to fight off the negative cycle that for a short time began to control my life.

The point was, I was reminding myself of positivity; things that existed within my life that gave me happiness and love. Simply thinking about these people gave me comfort and support, allowing me to ease my own critical judgement and condemnation. The repetitive action still existed in the form of me thinking of these people, saying their names in my head over and over, but it meant that instead of opening and closing the door 15 times, it was three or four times, until eventually, I could do it all in one motion. Eventually, I could even start using just the one name at a time to counter the pending negativity, like a flood barrier stopping a negative tidal wave of emotion crashing over me.

Even to this day I still sometimes need to use this technique. It works quite well for me. But it must be said that when I find myself needing to think in this way, it is a wakeup call that perhaps I'm not feeling so happy. So I take into action everything that I've learnt to help find my way back to the positive side of things, working on myself to improve my situation.

This technique helps me in those immediate moments when I'm becoming trapped in a cycle of negative thoughts and repetitive movements. It is also important to accept that any intrusive thoughts are involuntary and not your own. Acknowledge them, but accept them as a manifestation of your anxiety and let them go.

However, to fully take control of my life and make my OCD less of a debilitating or frequent occurrence, I still needed to work on my general mental health as a whole.

That means eating healthy to give myself the positive nutrients my body needs, drinking plenty of water to remove unwanted toxins from my system, and exercising to relieve tension and negative energy. I also make sure to go outside regularly to get fresh air and to speak to friends about how I feel. I would work on myself and try to improve each of the four pillars of my life to avoid coming back to this state of mind.

I need to maintain a healthy mind to minimise occurrences of OCD flare-ups. Now that my mental health is in a much better place, this is hardly ever an issue, but when I do start noticing that behaviour, it is a very quick wake-up call; a flashback that reminds me of how bad a state I was in before and how much I don't want to ever return to that place in my mind again. It motivates me to put in the work to ensure I keep a healthy and happy mind.

Lessons Learned

- If you experience uncontrollable repetitive behaviour or frequent intrusive thoughts that make you feel uneasy, you might have OCD, and you should seek advice from a professional.

- Obsessive-compulsive disorder is different for everyone, and what works for me might not work for you.

- Understand what an 'intrusive thought' is and don't overthink them. Learn to acknowledge and accept them as part of your anxiety and not a genuine thought, feeling, or reflection of yourself.

- My OCD was triggered by my depression and my anxiety. In the interim, saying the names of friends in my head helped me to counter my negative thoughts and end the repetitive motion cycles I got stuck in.

- If you experience OCD flare-ups, consider it a red flag that your mental health is not right. Make sure to address it, and do what you need to do to ease the stress and anxiety you are feeling.

- Ask for help and speak to a professional.

- Remember to eat healthy, drink plenty of water, and get regular exercise. Go outside and get fresh air regularly. Speak to your friends about how you feel.

Seasonal Affective Disorder

Now I can't say that I strictly suffer from seasonal affective disorder (SAD), but I do believe that I am usually feeling a little less motivated in the winter, and if things aren't going particularly well at that time, it does tend to exacerbate things. It amplifies the feeling of loneliness, and just the thought of getting out of bed in the morning while it is still dark outside is unappealing; discouraging even. The dark nights can feel empty when you have no one to go home to or few social plans to fill your week with.

The winter period is known to be a difficult time for the older age group too, especially around Christmas, when many can be left feeling very lonely. It can be a difficult season for a lot of people, and during my most trying times, the winter was always the hardest. In the summer or the springtime, getting some exercise and fresh air requires much less effort to muster. I have always associated myself with warmer climates. Whenever I've headed off on months-long backpacking adventures, they have always started in the European winter season.

Fortunately, while it is winter in Europe, it is summer (or at least much warmer and sunnier) in the southern hemisphere, so that is where I usually try to head. That is partly also why I moved to live in Barcelona, because even when things have not gone so well or I have struggled to set up the life that I wanted here, it is so much easier with all the sunny days to encourage me. Don't get me wrong; in the right moments I love the winter, whether it is during a ski/snow holiday with friends, a cuddle on the sofa whilst watching a movie with your partner, or a glass of mulled wine at the Christmas market.

There are many fun, loving, and cosy days and nights that can only happen in the winter. But for me, being here in a much sunnier place than my home back in England helps me to sustain a more constant positive mentality. I am much more content sitting on my balcony in the sunshine reading a book than being home in the British winter with nothing to do. Boredom sets in much more quickly, and that nagging reminder of being single or feeling alone pokes its ugly head up much more frequently on those cold, rainy, and dreary days and nights.

It can even be a natural way for you to realise that you are not happy in your home or your work life. Sitting in an office late at night whilst facing a dark and freezing walk home really makes you think about whether it is worth it or not. I would always look at my evenings differently in the winter. At 4 p.m. or 5 p.m., when the light begins to fade and you are still working towards the end of the working day, I'm less encouraged to make the most of the evening.

I just want to get home, put on my comfy sweatpants, and curl up on the sofa in the warmth.

Whereas in the spring or the summer, I'm eager to fill my calendar with drinks, dinners, and activities. Maybe being British gives me that extra urge to make the most of the sunshine, but I do look forward to the summer, and I dread its end. That feeling of dread can be so real that I worry whether I have made enough of the summer months. Did I really enjoy it to the fullest? Could I have done more? I long for those fun, sociable memories with family and friends, whether it is a family BBQ, a holiday abroad, drinks with friends in the beer garden, or a picnic at the beach; I enjoy it all.

Winter can still be fun and even magical, but I think that the summer is more forgiving if your plans fall through or you're having an off day. You will believe that you'll have another chance to make up for it because the sun will keep shining. But in the winter, it feels a little more unforgiving. Of course, this is a mindset, and finding a way to focus on the positives and to enjoy the unique winter experiences and magical moments can help you to shift your mentality to a more positive outlook.

If you know that you struggle in the winter, make sure you prepare for it. Make a plan to keep up your exercise and the stress-releasing activities that work so well for you in the summer. Actively arrange plans with family and friends, and keep those lines of communication open. Shift your summer holiday to the winter to break up those long nights with a bit of sunshine fun. Or if more drastic action is needed, you can always follow suit and move to a warmer climate. But as always, identifying this as an issue will allow you to better prepare yourself for a much easier winter season.

If you're aware that you struggle more during this time or you know that you suffer from seasonal affective disorder, don't ignore it. Don't put it off and wait for it to sneak up on you, catching you off guard and underprepared. Look ahead and make changes to your life to ensure you struggle less each year.

Working remotely is becoming more and more possible, so consider whether you can spend some of the time working at home during the winter to avoid those depressing commutes at the end of the day. You could even go abroad to brighten up those dark nights. If you are fortunate enough to have a more flexible way of working, perhaps you can work in the evening and be outside in the daytime to make the most of the winter sun. Flip the script. Change things up and make winter more fun and memorable. It doesn't have to be so difficult; we can choose to make it better. We can change our habits and our behaviours to promote a healthier mindset.

Lessons Learned

- Seasonal affective disorder is a real thing, and it affects many people. If you experience it, plan ahead and prepare yourself for the winter.

- Book your summer holiday in the winter. Organise events and make regular plans with friends and family.

- Make a conscious effort to stay fit and active. Exercise regularly.

- Keep your lines of communication open. Don't hide yourself away; keep talking to friends and family regularly.

- Work from home more if possible to avoid the commute. Work in a café or at a friend's house and break up the routine.

- Consider working abroad for a while.

- Try switching things up and make more of the daylight hours and work more in the evening.

Bad Things do Happen

I don't believe in fate. I don't believe that everything happens for a reason other than in the explainable 'cause and effect' way. I do not believe that certain things are destined to be; I believe that the decisions we and others make and the actions we take will shape our own and collective futures. But sometimes, the unexplainable happens. Call it 'chance,' coincidence, luck, or good fortune, but it is these moments that help us understand that we cannot control everything. Sometimes things will happen (good or bad) that we were not expecting and that we could not plan for.

The moment that stands out to me is the moment I lost my job as a young 21-year-old. It was only a temporary job in a local pub, and I hated it. It was a job I had taken out of pure necessity, having just quit another job I hated—working in a warehouse where I felt alone, unappreciated, and trapped in a future that looked professionally bleak. This was after years of volatility, the fallout from dropping out of university, and my heaviest state of depression. I was trying to find my way; trying to get myself out of a rut and on to a brighter path. And then the unthinkable happened.

I got fired from my pub job because well, I deserved it. I hated it and didn't want to be there, and the manager said as much. He simply said (in a nice and understanding way) that I didn't want to be there and so I should go home. I was a little shocked, upset, confused, and embarrassed, but also relieved. And I had no idea how much I would end up being thankful for it.

Losing that job meant that, years after my depression had taken hold of my life, I was still lost and still struggling, and now I had to try to find my way all over again. After driving home that day, I pulled up to my family home to find it empty. Instead of going in, throwing on the tv and distracting myself, I felt the compelling urge to go and visit my grandparents.

After all, I had been sent home from work early, so it was still a reasonable time to visit. What surprised me was that pretty much my entire family was at my grandparents', which was a little weird but not too unlikely, as my nan and my grandad always brought the family together. So, I dismissed it as a coincidence that they all happened to visit on the same day. But when I arrived my grandad summoned me. Well, he requested to see me because he knew something I could not comprehend. He was in bed because he had been struggling with a lung disease and was not at his strongest, but he was strong and stubborn like me, and he continued to make the most of his life. I assumed that he would be around for a lot longer still. I spoke with him that evening, and although I was feeling a little down, he gave me an immediate lift. He was my idol; the man I measured myself against and the person I wanted to be like: strong, caring, polite, funny, and a joy to be around.

At that moment, I did not understand the importance of our conversation, but I felt something deep down inside that I could not understand. I got to say goodbye to him that day, and it was only possible because I lost my job. I lost my job, and I then lost my grandad the next morning. I was beyond devastated. We all were. But after the tears began to subside and I was able to pick myself up again, it started to sink in. I had the chance to say goodbye. If I had not lost my job, I would have been the only one in the family not to have seen him that day, and I can't even begin to imagine what effect that may have had on me. Although I was not in the toughest period of my depression, I was still fragile. But instead of crumbling, I was able to hold enough of myself together because I found strength in the positivity that the universe had intervened and allowed me to have my final moment with my beloved grandfather—something I would never ever trade for anything.

We cannot always control what happens in our lives. Sometimes bad things do and will happen. It is a hard thing for us to accept, but the thing we need to remember is that no matter what happens, good things happen too. We can't let the bad things win, because often good things will come too. It may take time to uncover them; years for us to be able to see and appreciate them, but no matter what has happened in our past, there are good things in our present that wouldn't exist without them. Everything that has happened in our lives up unto this point has played a role in forging us, our relationships, and everything in our lives today.

Lessons Learned

- We can control a lot of what happens in our lives through the choices we make and the actions we take, but we cannot control everything.

- We cannot control the actions of others, and we cannot control mother nature, so let go of that responsibility because it is not yours to bear.

- Stop dreaming of fate intervening and take responsibility for what happens in your life.

- If you want something to change, it is up to you to change it.

- Remember that bad things do happen, but good things do too.

- Sometimes when bad things happen it works out for the best. You might not see it straight away, but it could end up being one of the best possible outcomes.

The Past Forms
the Present

'The past is the past' is a common phrase often thrown around without too much thought. At the heart of it, the sentiment is a positive one, but learning to accept this truth can also be a long and hard lesson to learn. I took a while for me to accept it because often I would find myself dwelling on the past. Mostly, I would focus on the bad things, the bad luck, the misfortune, the unfair treatment, the mistakes, and anything else that had disrupted my personal journey in a negative but memorable way.

This was especially true during my hardest times. During the peak of my depression, I would often replay the past over and over again in my head. Partly, this was because I'm a natural thinker. I would often analyse events in detail to consider all aspects, trying to understand what went wrong and why. Eventually, I would learn from my mistakes, but at the time I was just making myself feel worse; repeatedly replaying the negative events in my life like a broken record. It was just rubbing salt into the wounds, and it was slowing down my mental recovery. Nowadays I can let things go more quickly. I will learn what went wrong and have an understanding of why so that I can make sure it doesn't happen again, but I will learn from it, and most importantly, I know when to accept what cannot be changed.

The thing about the past is that it is time that has already passed. It cannot be done again. There is no point in beating yourself up thinking about and worrying about things that you cannot change.

When I look back now, I can understand and appreciate that no matter what I did differently, some things would still have (more or less) played out in the same way, and others were just outside of my control entirely.

But in my darkest days, I hated and resented myself for making poor choices, mistakes, and bad decisions. I would mentally punish myself; I would say angry and insulting things to myself to remind me of the mistakes that I'd made. I guess I wanted to make sure that I remembered the pain I had caused myself so that I wouldn't do it again, or perhaps there was no underlying reason other than shame and regret plaguing my thoughts. In my mind, I had let myself down. But further to this constant bombardment of negativity, I would fantasise about going back in time, reliving my life in a different way or in parallel universes where my life would be different. In some cases, only a few humble things would be different—maybe I would live the exact same life but with 30% more self-confidence, because I believed that was a handicap that had held me back. And that one change might have led to many different and more positive things happening.

Other times I dreamt about having chosen a different university and degree and living on campus with a loan and doing things the usual way. I'd fantasise about how that simple change would have enhanced my professional career, removing significant financial vulnerability and increasing my freedom of choice.

Whatever the scenario, the final thought was always the same. Yes, I could have done things differently, and yes, perhaps in some ways I could be better off. Maybe my mental health struggles would have been less intense. The fact is, I can never know how things could have or would have turned out. What I do know is that, had I made different choices or taken a different path, I would have had many amazing experiences, but there are people that I most likely would never have met and friendships that I would not have forged. And no matter how much I look back, I would never want to sacrifice the lasting friendships that I have gained or my most special memories I have created since.

No matter how hard your journey has been, it has shaped you into who you are today, including all the good things we and others love about ourselves. I understand that the difficult mental health experiences that I had have helped to create a very strong person with some real wisdom and life experience that I can use to help others. Experiences that help me to understand what others might be going through, to never take anything for granted, and to find greater empathy for others. I will try my best to never overlook someone else's problems and to be there for my friends and family when they need me, as best as I can be. Sharing all of the positives and the negatives. I am now fully equipped to deal with whatever life throws at me. I know that I have been through the wars, and I have repeatedly picked myself up and continued forward. Because of my experiences, I am who I am: a strong-willed man who is brave and resilient, and I am proud of that.

The only way to stop overanalysing and worrying about the past is to accept it for what it is. You have to reframe your thoughts and consider all that you have gained. Think about all the good things you would lose if you somehow undid what happened in your life.

Life is full of endless interconnected moments, and any change to your past would likely erase everything that has happened since. There is no way to change the past and certainly no way to change it while keeping all the good things. Think about what you have gained since then; what have you learnt. The strengths you have gained, the relationships you've built, and the moments you've enjoyed. Yes, it was bad and it's ok to remember how it felt, but remember that you survived it; you are here thinking back to it. You've made it this far and you'll make it further. You have survived everything that happened, and you are strong enough to accept it and move forward.

Acknowledge that you have to let go of what happened so you can heal, move forward, and make the most of your life. You do not have to forget it, but forgive yourself for it; forgive life for it. Focus on the here and the now. Focus on your future and the things that you can control. Remember, bad things do happen, but so good things. Let go of what you can't control and focus on what you can. The past has helped shape who you are today, and the present will shape who you are in the future.

Lessons Learned

- You need to let go of the past to be truly present in the present.

- You can't change the past, no matter how much you wish for it.

- Focus on everything you have gained since then. Changing the past would mean sacrificing every relationship you've made and every positive experience you've had since then.

- Take the lessons learnt from the past and embrace the here and the now.

- Everything that has happened has led you to the person you are today. All the hard times really do make you a stronger person.

A Little Bit of Showboating Goes a Long Way

Sometimes, a little bit of showboating can go a long way. Not in a disrespectful or egotistical way, but by actually enjoying the little successes. Especially if you are someone who is quite self-deprecating, overtly modest, wickedly shy, struggling with insecurity and low self-esteem, or someone who is so focused on others that they forget to appreciate themselves. Remember when you were a child, living carefree? Remember how you would celebrate any win or achievement as a moment of genuine passion and pride?

I remember playing football with my friends almost every day, and whenever someone scored a goal, they would celebrate like crazy. If you scored a particularly good goal, you would go absolutely bananas, imitating your favourite players' celebrations and genuinely enjoying the moment. It is only as you get older that you become more self-conscious of celebrating; people tend to grow jealous or resentful. What had been a purely innocent moment of pride and passion in childhood becomes gloating and unsportsmanlike as an adult. And so, when you start to become more self-aware of your actions and don't want to be thought of as inconsiderate, you start to suppress those genuine feelings of happiness. And over time you understandably grow out of such celebrations, becoming more conscious of being respectful to others. But sometimes you might deprive yourself of really enjoying those little moments of pride and elation.

What a shame to waste such pure happiness. Whether you have just bested your friend who always beats you at a game of FIFA, finally mastered a TikTok dance routine you've been working on for weeks, created a new cooking recipe, or gotten a promotion at work—why not celebrate? Have your moment, be a little silly, bounce around on your bed, tease your friend (in jest and good nature); really enjoy it and let it sink in. Your friends and family will enjoy seeing you happy, and the feeling will last that little bit longer. We all enjoy seeing people happy because it makes us happy too. One smile attracts another; happiness is infectious.

Sometimes a little self-indulgence can go a long way to lift your mood. I remember a few years ago when I was playing football in central London under the spotlights, I scored an incredible volley from the halfway line. But as the ball hit the back of the net, I didn't hear an immediate cheer (like you would expect), so I quickly stunted my celebration and doubted what had just happened. I was thinking that if I celebrated too much it would be out of place, but as I looked up, I saw the shock and disbelief on people's faces, and then the congratulations started to roll in. But by then, I had suppressed my own joy too much to really enjoy what

I had just done. I was so conscious of others that I missed the chance to celebrate a once in a lifetime goal. The eight-year-old me would have been bemused and disappointed; he would have been going crazy with joy, so why didn't I? It is good to be a considerate person, but not to the expense of your own happiness.

Nobody would judge you for celebrating your success. Take pride in yourself and enjoy your achievements; big or small. Soak up the positivity and boost your self-esteem.

This feeling of self-conscious behaviour isn't isolated to limiting our joyous moments of success. It can also affect us on regular occasions. For instance, vanity or self-care is a bit of a minefield. On one side of the spectrum, someone can become a little self-obsessed and egotistical, and on the other, they can be damagingly critical of themselves. And somewhere in the middle of it all is a confusion of conflicted feelings.

For me, this might mean that on a day—when I believe I'm looking good, I have dressed well, and I'm feeling confident—I can find myself in a bar with friends or out in public somewhere walking around with a cheeky smile on my face and a bit of swagger. I can almost feel my own confidence as if it was a tangible entity, like an aura radiating out of me from within. Whilst riding high on a wave of self-confidence I can find myself seeking a little more of the spotlight than usual, making jokes, & leading conversations. I will then take further energy, confidence, and reassurance from other people engaging with me positively, encouraged by the laughs at my jokes or the positive eye contact I'm receiving. But then I might catch myself and question my actions or my body language: Am

I being overconfident? Am I trying to steal the spotlight from my friends or seeking too much attention?

I might question my own integrity a little, thinking I'm being obnoxious by allowing my confidence to flow and perhaps I need to reign it in. I will then quickly lose that feeling of confidence and start to feel a little self-conscious. I will adjust my behaviour by stopping myself from making a joke or stunt my desire to say something while I consider how I am being perceived by the group to ensure I haven't overstepped the mark.

There's nothing wrong with being a little self-conscious or self-aware of your actions and how they impact others, but that shouldn't deprive you of feeling good. There is no harm in being a little cheeky; walking with your head held high or wanting to participate in conversations and share the spotlight for a moment.

We shouldn't feel guilty for having such a visceral physiological reaction to positive engagement. We are allowed to feel confident, to feel good about how we look, and to enjoy some attention and the positive energy that comes back to us. We are allowed to be an active participant in any social activity we want to indulge in. It is good to be self-aware, but we should still allow ourselves to enjoy the moment. Especially if you usually struggle with your self-confidence or you're in need of a little lift to your mood.

Allowing yourself to feel a sense of pride for being confident and outgoing might even enable you to overcome some other issues, like meeting new people. Those little moments may lead to other moments that perhaps wouldn't happen if you suppressed those natural feelings. Because when you stop yourself from feeling that confidence, pride, or joy, you make way for negativity instead, doubting yourself and questioning your natural instinctive feelings and reactions.

Furthermore, a related area of complication is taking pride in your appearance (something that is often over-scrutinised). Consider the invention of the selfie as an example. For some, it simply gave them the opportunity to take a picture of a positive moment and to share it with their friends without having to feel insecure or self-conscious about asking a stranger for assistance. For some, it was liberation. But it then started to be associated with ego and vanity. I personally always found it hard to ask a stranger to take a picture for me, and because of the bad rep selfies were getting, I then found it embarrassing to take one. So instead, I mostly excluded myself from my own photo memories to avoid the embarrassment altogether. Rather than focusing on the positive moment I wanted to capture, I was caught up in the social awkwardness of it all.

I cared too much about what others might think rather than feeling free to enjoy things without judgement. If you want to take a picture of yourself because you are happy with the way you look or because you want to capture a moment or a feeling; go for it. Stop worrying about what other people think. Enjoy those moments without worry and celebrate yourself.

Now consider another scenario, like going to the beach. It is normal for people to show a lot of skin there, but for a long time I never really felt totally at ease with being so exposed. In my teenage years, I was quite self-critical of my physical appearance. I felt insecure about my weight, I thought that I was too thin, and I resented a part of myself for it. But I was a fussy eater at the time, and at that age I had very little control over what I ate. With little personal income and your family meals prepared for you, you stick with what is familiar and easy.

As I got older and braver and I began to try new foods, I started eating more. As an adult, I invested in myself and went to work in the gym to build my body. And it worked. My self-confidence started to grow, but for a long time I still felt uneasy about taking my shirt off at the beach. But now it was less about being insecure with how I looked and more about vanity. It goes back to that confidence scenario: How do I feel if someone is looking at my body? Am I allowed to feel proud about how I look or is that egotistical?

I now felt comfortable and confident in my own body, but I wasn't allowing myself to feel that way. I felt like I was being judged, and so what should be a happy occasion was somewhat marred by this internal process. The old me felt exposed and vulnerable, and the new me felt like any feeling of pride would mean that I was shallow and egotistical.

Instead, I should have been able to appreciate the hard work I had put in to transform my body from a source of insecurity to a source of pride and confidence. We're allowed to take pride in the way we look, and we're allowed to celebrate the hard work we have put into something without worrying about the judgement of others. As long as we are being respectful and considerate of others, we can stop questioning ourselves so much and enjoy things a little more.

We should be more accepting of self-love and self-appreciation. It's good to take pride in and to feel good about yourself. Especially when it comes to our bodies, given the negative criticism and abuse that people often suffer online, especially women. This is an unhealthy environment we have created. We need to instead support our friends and encourage them to feel good about themselves. Being conscious of your own outward projection and your impact on others is an evolved stated of being, but we should cut ourselves a little slack too.

Life is hard enough without us constantly scrutinizing our every move. If you want to take a selfie because you feel good today and you want to share that with your friends online, then why not? Friendships are our support network, so we should encourage each other to appreciate ourselves. Love yourself and enjoy your moments of success. Allow yourself to feel pride and be happy. Release your inner child and live a little more carefree.

Lessons Learned

- Remember what it was like to be a child and to be carefree, and embrace your inner child.

- Enjoying the little moments makes life more enjoyable. So enjoy them, celebrate your successes, and be proud of who you are.

- Allow yourself those moments of joy. Let go of your inhibitions and set free yourself free. Be silly and enjoy the little moments.

- A little bit of ego is ok. It is healthy for you to take pride in your appearance and feel good about how you look.

Be in the Moment

Enjoy the little things. The best thing about getting older is that you learn to care a little less about what other people think of you. You start to appreciate the little things a lot more and learn to embrace your eccentricities without feeling the judgement of others. It is so freeing as a 30-something man to not care about what others might think if I'm at home on a Friday night watching a Disney movie. What do I care if someone else thinks it is uncool? That's for them to wallow in their negativity while I enjoy what makes me happy. Listen to the music you want to listen to, even if it isn't what is trending at the moment. Wear what makes you feel good. Be true to yourself and worry less about what others think, because stressing over what they might be thinking and applying their judgements to yourself internally isn't helpful. You have no idea what most people are actually thinking, and you may never know, so you are making assumptions based on your own insecurities and fears, which is only harming yourself and not them. You are causing your own suffering. You are preventing yourself from just being you. You need to let go of what you cannot control, especially the thoughts of other human beings.

This is something that I try to remind myself of all the time; to enjoy things more, to be in the moment, and to stop worrying about what others might think or what comes next. One thing that I realised early on was that I loved travelling and photography, but when I recall my early travels, I remember taking so many photos it was ridiculous. I was never going to see them all, and if I think back to some of the places I went to, I probably spent too long worrying about taking the perfect picture rather than just enjoying the moment. I learnt to put the camera away, take a few snaps, and then give myself some time to take in my surroundings. I needed to force myself to take a moment and appreciate the view or fall fully into the occasions and genuinely enjoy it. After all, the photos will last, but they will mean a lot more if they remind you of real memories that you created and captured rather than just a nice picture.

Perhaps it is the age of the influencer, but there are so many people out there spending so much time stressing over the best photo that they miss out on what's important. You can look back at over 1,000 photos, but if you didn't create a real tangible memory, they will just be pretty pictures.

Social media is another source of influence; there is so much negativity on the internet, and if you are not careful, it can take over. The accounts that you follow and the posts that you read can all subtly influence your mood each day. I only follow intelligent, kind, positive people who share similar views or passions to mine. I remove, block, or ignore the negatives and focus on the positives.

Social media can be a good thing when it is used right, so it is important to remind yourself that you have complete control and power in that environment. You can selectively curate your own little world filled with positivity.

It is also good to remember that when you're having a tough time, you shouldn't get too caught up in how others are living; it isn't all sunshine and rainbows. People mostly post only their best moments, so that's all you get to see. You don't see their actual everyday lives. Having travelled a lot myself, I know that there are a many difficult moments to go with the amazing times and plenty of sacrifices made along the way. Even the biggest travel bloggers and lifestyle influencers will have their difficult moments. They just don't share them online because they wouldn't get enough likes or follows.

You have to remember that most influencers are running a business and creating a brand, and so they have to carefully select each post to keep their audience happy and engaged in their content. It isn't worth comparing yourself to someone's social media persona; it may be very different from their real life. Many influencers work extremely hard to live their lives the way they do. Waking up at 3 a.m. to get to a destination before anybody else just to take one photo isn't everyone's ideal lifestyle. We need to learn to take a lot of it at face value and not to compare it to our own lives. Instead, follow the people you think are most genuine and who contribute something positive to your life.

Even outside of social media, it is good to apply the same rules to life. If you want to be happy, you need to keep positive people around you; friends and family who actually care about you; people who will give you their time, who are happy to support you and listen to you, and who you can be yourself around.

Growing up you don't realise it, but when you get older you notice that so many connections you make along the way may have been good at the time, but you were never really that deeply bonded. You realise that you had plenty of people in your life who didn't share your views or didn't challenge you in a positive way; people who you wouldn't choose to be friends with if you had to go to a store to pick them out. As you get older, it becomes more obvious, as it is harder to keep in touch with people as their lives progress. You start being a little more honest with yourself and you learn to say no to people a little more.

It is ok to choose not to spend time with someone you don't really like or see a long future with. If you don't enjoy someone's company or they make you feel uncomfortable, you shouldn't feel pressured or obliged to spend time with them. I'm obviously not suggesting that you make snap judgements, but when you've spent a bit of time with people, you usually know if you have a good feeling around them or not. Your friendship group will always shrink over time. As you get older, you discover who really cares; the people who make the effort to remain a part of your life. Those are the ones to embrace and enjoy life with.

I try to adopt the holiday mode in my everyday life as much as I can; that go-with-the-flow mentality. When I'm travelling or on holiday, my overall mood doesn't get affected by bad luck or negativity. I just shrug it off because I'm so happy to be free. Letting go of your stress, work, and other things is so hard to do but so beneficial when you can do it. Walking out of work at 5 p.m. or whenever you finish and forgetting the day is so good for you. However you let go of the stress, whether you can just switch your focus or you need to exercise, meditate, listen to music, have a laugh with a friend, or watch something, it is good to release that stress as soon as you can. Stress is something that continually builds up, so you need a reliable way to process those emotions and let them go so you can enjoy the here and now without feeling tense or anxious.

Sometimes it is hard to let go of things, but I always value the 'sleep on it' philosophy. Tomorrow is a new day; I can sleep away the pain, shame, stress, or regret and start afresh tomorrow, like respawning or restarting a video game. I can start over with a fresh new perspective and fully recharged energy reserves. Sometimes I just accept that there is nothing I can do today. Today I feel sad, but tomorrow I can try again. I allow myself to feel down; to have that time to process my emotions, and then tomorrow I wake up and take action to ensure I don't feel like that again. That's what you do when you restart or respawn in a video game. You try something different and push yourself forward to complete the next level having learnt from your previous attempts.

Another thing I became aware of is that through all my depression and negativity, I found myself reflecting too much. I was always worrying, always focusing on the negatives and never really being fully present. I guess I was experiencing the act of mindfulness before I knew what it was. I became more aware of who I was and what I was doing at different moments. Sometimes when I was with friends, I found myself passively listening rather than being actively present in the conversation. Whilst listening, I could be selfishly thinking about how what they were saying affected me, what to say next, or still partially focusing on the issues in my life rather than being there for the other person.

I learnt that I needed to let go of what has already happened (the past is the past) and to not dwell on what others might or might not be thinking. I needed to be mindful of myself and the situation; to let go of what I cannot control so that I can be fully present in the moment. Not only is it more polite to the other person if you are actively listening, but it can also help to distract yourself from your own worries. Making a conscious effort to listen to what someone is saying is a good trait to have. I haven't mastered it, but I'm always aware of when I'm fully engaged or not, and I'm sure my conversation partners are too. After all, I have a face that struggles to hide what I'm really thinking; it is a gift and a curse. But is an area that I'm working on, and it is something we should consider. Are we giving the other person the attention they deserve? Are we being mindful of the situation at hand and our role within it?

The act of mindfulness is a good habit to practice. You can start by taking a deep breath and calming yourself before starting something new. Take a walk, listen to some music, and clear your mind. Talk to someone about what's bothering you and give yourself that outlet so it isn't taking over your mind all the time. Then you can ask yourself questions. When you're taking a photo, you can ask yourself if you have taken enough and if you should perhaps focus on enjoying the moment. In a conversation, you can ask yourself if you are really listening. Did you hear what they just said? Are you matching their energy and showing them that you are listening? It's about being aware of what's happening and reminding yourself of what you are meant to be doing in that moment.

Social media and the perception of others got me thinking about what makes a person 'cool.' What is this benchmark that we compare ourselves to so regularly? Being cool is not about wearing the latest fashion trends or speaking in the latest lingo. You can slang yourself away with the freshest words and swagger with the latest threads as much as you like, but it won't make you cool. A person who you are most likely to perceive as cool, likeable, and charismatic, is someone who is happy within themselves. Someone who is being real, doing what they want to do, and enjoying life.

The reason why most genuinely cool people make it look so effortless is because it is. We do idolise self-love; we just don't realise it. We are drawn to naturally confident people; open and honest people, because that's what we really value: being true to ourselves and allowing ourselves to be happy. That's how you enjoy life and the people in it. Not the fakers or the posers, but real people being real. Embracing who you are; all of your strengths, all of your weaknesses, your successes, and your failures. All of your eccentricities, popular or not. Just be yourself.

When you're able to let go of your insecurities and allow yourself to be present in the moment, you can really start to enjoy life as you experience it rather than retrospectively.

Lessons Learned

- Be in the moment and enjoy the little things. Enjoy what makes you happy without worrying about what other people think.

- You cannot control the thoughts inside other people's heads, and you have no idea what they are really thinking. Any assumptions you make are based on your own fears and insecurities, not reality.

- Don't worry about people judging you. They might not even be doing it, and it will have little or no consequence if they do.

- You're allowed to choose your friends, so choose wisely. Surround yourself with those who contribute positively to your life, and remove the toxic people from it.

- Remember that social media is only a glimpse of reality and is rarely a reflection of real life.

- Curate your social media; you have full control of it. Follow only those who are a source of positivity.

- Embrace the sleep-on-it mentality. Allow yourself to feel down when you need to, but remind yourself that tomorrow is a new day and you can start with a refreshed mind.

- Go with the flow. Things happen, and you can't control everything.

- Practice the art of mindfulness. Be present in the moment and be aware of your surroundings. Ask yourself questions to make sure you are focused on the here and now.

- Be an active listener. Be engaged and present when in conversation with someone.

Nature Heals

Go to the top of a mountain. Not metaphorically, but literally go there. Go for a hike in nature. Stand there at the top of a mountain and just look. Look at the beauty all around you. Listen to the sounds of nature. Breathe and let the peace and tranquillity calm you. Feel what it is to be alive. Scream if you have to. Let it all out and admire the world around you.

Immersing yourself in nature is an amazing way to find peace, to refresh your mind and your soul, and to remind yourself what life is really about. It is not about the hustle and bustle of modern-day life; it is about finding peace and happiness in all of the things around you. Enjoy the immense beauty of this incredible planet we are fortunate to live on.

I lived in London during the better half of my 20s. It was a fast-paced life, and it sometimes felt like everyone was out for themselves, fighting their way to the top. You work hard and you play hard. It is all go, go, go. Having so much going on in every pillar of your life can be stressful. It is certainly hard work, but it is also fun and enjoyable to live in one of the greatest cities in the world. But there comes a point when you start to get a little tired. Tired of working all-out for little reward. The corporate world of office politics, Monday to Friday routines, excessive overtime, and pressure and stress eventually get old.

After a while, even with a hectic social life, you begin to realise that you're not necessarily getting as much out of your life as you are putting into it. And the moment you take a break, slow things down, escape the city, and explore what the world has to offer, you realise that you can find a lot of joy and happiness in the simple tranquillity of nature. I think it is in those moments when you leave a busy period of your life that you really notice the power of nature. It is that contrast of lifestyles that makes it stand out.

Think about when you've had a particularly busy or stressful period in your life and you've taken a much-needed break or gone on holiday somewhere scenic. All you need to be happy is to relax with family or friends. You can enjoy a nice cool breeze on a warm summer day; it is calm, relaxing, and genuine happiness. Think about when you go to the beach and you hear the sounds of the waves on the shore. You take a walk across the sand and feel the water wash over your toes. You feel the warmth of the sun on your skin and hear the sounds of kids playing and people laughing in the distance. It really doesn't take much to be happy.

When you're chilling in a hammock, falling asleep under the rustling of palm tree leaves, listening to the sounds of the water on the shore and the birds in the trees; what are you thinking about? Anything? You are probably not thinking about work, money, politics, or technology. I'm going to go out on a limb and say you're probably thinking something like "Man, I wish every day could be like this."

It is so easy to get wrapped up in the craziness of life. There is so much social pressure to live your life in a certain way. The modern society we live in today is built on this model of growth and success. You're encouraged to seek the next promotion, to get a bigger house, to buy more expensive clothes, get the latest technology, and everything else. It is easy to get lost in the chase for the next level of things.

Sometimes we have to remind ourselves of why we are actually here. It is good to have dreams and goals and to progress your career and elevate your life, as long as you don't miss out on appreciating it while you live it. Nature reminds us of this.

I'd happily trade any career to spend the rest of my life relaxing with friends and family outside enjoying the mountains, the ocean, and the beauty of nature. Obviously, that isn't a realistic option, but it is possible to make more of nature and to appreciate life more just by making it a part of your weekly routine to go for walks outside, to play a sport, or to take the time to sit and chill in your garden or the local park. There is something so peaceful and calming about listening to the sounds of the wind in the trees, running water, or the animals communicating with one another. It is a great way to disconnect from stress; to take a moment to breathe and relax the muscles. The more time we spend out in nature, the better we feel.

Enjoying nature was always a big part of my travels. When I went away to Asia or South America for four months, the freedom and adventure helped me to enjoy life and create some special memories. But it was nature that made me fall in love with travel and to fall in love with life again. Those days relaxing on the beach helped me to remove a lot of stress and negativity from my life, and those days hiking up mountains showed me the value of hard work and the beauty that exists all around us. Those were some of the happiest days of my life.

I remember mountain biking down a hill with my friend to the river at the bottom of a valley. I remember standing still and quiet as we watched a family of deer run across the river. I remember those moments more vividly than any day working or going out for drinks in the city.

There is something about nature that really connects with your soul. My memories of standing on the top of a mountain in the middle of Yosemite National Park in California when I was 20 years old fill me with joy, and if I close my eyes, I can still transport myself back there. I can see the snow-capped mountains in the distance. I can feel the wind on the back of my neck as I look across the valley to El Capitan and let my eyes survey the land in awe as they reach the waterfalls in the distance. Those memories eclipse years of my career or everyday life.

It's good to have ambitions; to work hard and chase your dreams, but it is also good to take a moment to appreciate life. The more time you spend outdoors, the happier you will feel. A city break is fun, but consider taking at least one holiday a year that lets you disconnect and enjoy nature. Go on a hike, take a horse ride along the hillside, or relax on the beach. Allow both your body and your mind some time to disconnect from the stresses of everyday life and reconnect with the world around you. Break up the weekly routine and spend time with friends and family outdoors. Play more sport, go for walks, or enjoy a picnic in the park.

Not only does nature help relax the soul and soothe stress, but it helps you to heal. I remember being in New Zealand towards the end of my travels back when I was 24 years old. I had travelled on my own for four months across two continents, and I'd had my ups and my downs. I had spent a few days unwell and was feeling lonely and beginning to worry about my return home to 'reality.' It was making me feel down, so I went for a walk through the trees and I found this bench overlooking the lake. I sat there for an hour or two and dealt with my emotions. I cried a little while the beauty around me comforted me and reminded me that everything was going to be ok.

It was hard for my fears to consume me while staring out at a beautiful lake surrounded by mountains. Nature gave me the strength to deal with my emotions. It allowed me the time and peace to process how I felt, and then it reminded me how incredible this place is. I always find it easier to get through the tough periods of my life when I spend more time outside in the countryside. It won't fix your problems; we still have to put in the work and give ourselves time, but it does help reduce stress and anxiety. It reminds you of the positive sides of life and of what's really important.

Life is hard, and it is so easy to get caught up in this idea of wanting more; always focusing on the next promotion, a bigger house, the next relationship milestone, and the next social occasion. We can get lost in our chase of the latest technology; the desire to upgrade our belongings or to reach another level of comfort or luxury. If we're not careful, time will pass us by without us creating many of those truly memorable moments that will last a lifetime. We can't get time back, so let's remember to appreciate our surroundings and immerse ourselves in nature. As human beings, we really don't need a lot to be happy. We need food, water, and shelter to survive. We need each other for companionship, and the rest already exists in nature.

The world is a truly magnificent place, and I have been fortunate enough to enjoy some of the most spectacular places on earth. I understand its power. So, get out there and enjoy the world you live in. There are so many incredible experiences waiting for you.

Lessons Learned

- Spending time in nature is great a way to destress and disconnect from everyday life and ease your anxiety.

- Spend more time outside; make it part of your weekly routine.

- Break up your year with holidays in nature. Go for a hike in the mountains, go horse riding along the hillside, or relax by the beach.

- It doesn't take much to be happy, so don't get too caught up in the chase for bigger and better things. Slow down and enjoy life.

- Memories in nature last longer than the hustle and bustle of everyday life.

- We live in the most incredibly beautiful world, so get out there and experience it first-hand.

Travel

To travel is to free your true self. It sounds a little cliché, but it is an important lesson that I learnt a long time ago. Modern society isn't designed to allow you to discover who you really are. Instead you're expected to conform and contribute before you even know what you are capable of. Native tribal groups understand this better than we do. For instance, the Aborigines in Australia are known for their practice of a Walkabout. Although aimed specifically at men as a rite of passage into adulthood, it is a practice that makes sense. Young men aged 10 to16 are sent off into the wild to fend for themselves for up to six months. In today's modern society, for many there is no such thing. Instead, you are sent off to explore the everyday stresses of life with very little preparation. Travelling/backpacking is essentially a modern alternative; taking a gap year or a long portion of time out from everyday society to travel the world and experience other cultures. It is a way of testing yourself and preparing yourself to become a responsible adult whilst also creating some of the best memories of your life.

Typically, as a backpacker, you are forced to live off of a pretty tight budget, and when travelling alone, you are forced to be the sole decision-maker. It is down to you to organise all your own accommodation and transport, and to be the sole navigator and the only person you can rely on in an emergency. It is not quite as treacherous as a 10-year-old boy heading off into the wild with nothing but his wits and intuition, but it does certainly pose some challenges and experiences that you may not otherwise have to deal with.

The experience of long-term travel isn't always Instagram worthy. There will be many tough days and lonely days. You may face genuine danger, or you may get lost. You will likely have to deal with stressful situations by yourself whilst trying to communicate with another culture in a foreign language. The cliché of finding oneself is because of all of this. You are free to be yourself for months on end without having to pretend to be someone else, to do as you are told, or to conform to routine and financial responsibility. You are testing yourself every day, & you're forced to face situations and challenges you may otherwise avoid. You will learn a lot more about yourself than most people do in years of normal life.

This is why I fell in love with traveling. I was lost, depressed, and confused. I didn't know who I was or what I was going to do with my life. Having dropped out of university with no plan B, I had spent the last year or two of my life in turmoil, drowning in self-hate and negativity. These dark feelings would often manifest themselves into snappy outbursts or tears.

The timing of my first backpacking adventure was crucial (I was 20 years old). At the time it felt like it may have saved my life; it was such an important intervention, and it was redefining. It allowed me to free myself from the worries and stress of the life I had found myself in. Instead, I could relax, breathe, and enjoy my freedom to experience life every day. I could do whatever I wanted. I had control, even if it was only temporary. I had the time to think. I learnt how to be an adult, I grew in confidence and self-assurance, and I had time to consider my future in detail without panic or fear clouding my mind. I no longer felt trapped, and I no longer felt the pressure from my family, my friends, society, or myself.

During the trip, I found myself outside of my comfort zone almost every day. I had to speak to strangers every day, and I had to figure out where I was going and what I was doing. I had to learn to be responsible and manage my budget, organise my accommodation, and navigate my way around a foreign country. I developed new skills and found an inner confidence that had been beaten down by my struggles back home. I made mistakes and learnt to remain calm. I even began to appreciate that the hardest days with the toughest challenges and the most mistakes would always become the most memorable moments and the best stories to tell.

And let's not forget the best part; being free of the normal responsibility of work, rent, bills, relationships, and more, means that you can actually enjoy life in the way you want to live it. You get to choose where you are going and what you are doing. You can pursue your passions and free your adventurous side.

Travelling is a cliché because it is incredibly fun, fulfilling, and memorable; that part is also true. It is the closest we ever come to living life to its fullest, outside of the limitations of society's rule and conformation. You are free to do whatever you want (within your budget obviously). One day you might hike up a mountain and take in some of the most incredible views you'll ever see. The next you might be meeting new friends in a buzzing new city or learn to surf with the locals on a quiet hidden beach. The next day you could be enjoying the magic of a beautiful sunset, having sex with the most beautiful person you've ever met, snorkelling with a turtle, or swimming with sharks. You might try authentic cuisine cooked fresh by a local or experience a local tradition or holiday. The list of possibilities is truly endless. I've done all of these things and more. I have more memories from a few months of travel than I will ever have from a year of normal life.

This is why I love to travel. I have so much more life experience because of it. I am a better and happier person because of it. I can appreciate different cultures and customs from all over the world; I've made friends from all corners of it. I've discovered myself. Sustained periods outside of my comfort zone have forced me to grow and mature so much more than I would have without it. Every trip I took filled me with newfound vigour. I would always come back with purpose and drive, and positive changes would usually follow.

A general misconception that exists is that travel is ridiculously expensive and out of reach for many people, but it doesn't have to be. My first trip across the USA (back in 2006) for two months cost me £3,500 in total.

That included flights, accommodation, travel, a helicopter ride, a limo rental, American football tickets, ice hockey tickets, museum tours, hiking, camping, and more.

My four-month trip around Thailand, Singapore, Australia, and New Zealand cost me £7,500 and included much of the same as well as snorkelling, scuba diving, sky diving, bungee jumping, and everything else. To put that into perspective, a weekend city break would often cost me around £350 all in (or more), and that's for only three days away. So, £3.5k for 20 times more days away at a cost of only 10 times the amount makes financial sense.

In a standard month in the UK or Spain, I would spend £1,200 to £1,800 as a minimum just for living (rent, food, travel, bills). If you can travel between rental contracts or rent out your own place while you're away, your financial responsibilities back home will be fairly manageable. I sublet my room and took a sabbatical from work. I worked overtime, cut back on alcohol and meals out, and reduced my other expenses over the course of a few months to save up the funds to travel. It wasn't easy, but a few small sacrifices here and there helped me to gain experiences that changed my life forever.

But travel isn't for everyone, so I would always go back to my point of just giving yourself a mental break. A few days or a couple of weeks is never enough. It is common practice here in Barcelona for most citizens to take three or four weeks off in August every year. A substantial break like that allows you to fully disconnect from work and relax; to enjoy yourself and your freedom and have genuine time to think and reflect on your life. It also allows for enough time to reconnect with family and friends.

After the global lockdowns of 2020, I think most people have come to identify the benefits of spending more time with loved ones than at work or in the hustle and bustle of everyday life. Sabbaticals, secondments, unpaid leave, extended holidays, or gap years are all things we should find a way to fit into our lives at one point or another. Life is stressful. It is full of pressure, expectation, responsibility, and all kinds of challenges, so whatever you can do to reduce this or to take regular breaks from it the better. Work, bills, and commitments are always going to be a part of society, but unless you're fortunate enough to have a job you love or a fulfilling, stress-free personal life, we might be missing out on the best bits. So, why wait until you retire? By then you'll have already missed a huge chunk of life and possibilities.

Seeing and experiencing other countries and cultures have helped me to fall in love with this amazing planet. The views of nature that I have seen with my own eyes, the man-made experiences I've had, the kindness of strangers that I have benefitted from, the new friends that I've made, the new foods that I've tried, and the wildlife I have immersed myself in have been absolutely breathtaking and beyond measure. I believe that despite all my difficulties—my troubles, my struggles, and my despair—I have still managed to live an incredible life full of incredible experiences, and I made it all happen. From my hard work and sacrifice, the risks I've taken, and the choices I've made, I have lived life to the fullest. I will always find great pride and power in that.

Lessons Learned

- In modern life we lack that natural rite of passage that forces us to discover who we are, test our limits, and learn to appreciate life.

- Traveling is the modern-day equivalent of a Walkabout.

- It is good for the soul to take a significant break away from everyday stress and societal pressure.

- Travelling takes you outside of your comfort zone every day. It helps you to learn who you are, what your strengths are, and what you are capable of.

- It can help you to grow as a person and to develop skills you otherwise wouldn't have the opportunity to.

- It can help you to put life into perspective and enjoy the little things more.

- You learn to appreciate other cultures and to consider new perspectives.

- You get to experience life at its best & create memories that will last a lifetime.

Financial Stress

Money is a bit perplexing when you think about it. It carries so much weight and value in our current society, even though it was introduced as a simple and fair mechanism for ensuring the equal distribution of things. Nowadays, it is a significant cause of stress and anxiety. Money can often cause feelings of shame or guilt about your spending or your earnings.

There is a lot of pressure to earn money; not just to pay for essential things like a home to live in (which gets harder every year), but to earn what is considered a 'good standard of living.' Money can often impact your mental health negatively in different ways.

We can feel guilt or shame about how much money we have wasted or how much we earn. For a long portion of my adult life, I struggled with financial shame. I felt embarrassed by how little I was earning, and I often compared myself to my friends. Having not completed a degree, I started my career in an entry-level position, and so when my friends started working, they were already earning considerably more than me. It wasn't until about the age of 28 to 30, when my career reached a similar level as that of my friends, that I started to let go of that shame.

I don't measure myself against others now, but back then I did. How much I got paid was always a source of stress and anguish. I always felt like I wasn't where I should have been, and I felt limited by what I could afford to do. I felt embarrassed when my friends wanted to do something that cost more money than I was comfortable with.

This is something that affects a lot of people, especially at Christmas. There is a lot of pressure around Christmas to spend money on food for hosting, gifts for friends and family, and the office Secret Santa. Not to mention the extra costs of all the social occasions on top of paying your usual bills and cost of living. Millions of people go into debt each Christmas because they feel pressured into spending. Even the act of exchanging gifts can cause anxiety as you wait for their reaction. You can feel self-conscious or guilty about how much you spent compared to the other person.

There was a time when I was self-conscious about how others perceived me in terms of money. I felt as though some of my friends judged me and thought me to be stingy. Perhaps it was guilt, but I always felt apprehensive or uneasy when spending money. I was very much aware of the value of my money and conscious that I have always had to work hard to have it. I was raised to work and earn my own money to pay for things from a young age.

When I was 12 years old, I helped my older brother out with his paper round, and he gave me £1 a week to help, so I was able to save that money up to buy the album cassette of the Spice Girls and Five. That's right, I had great taste. So as I grew up, I didn't always feel comfortable spending money so frivolously. I always thought through my purchases in detail. If I buy this for x amount, I can't buy this other thing. That's why I would spend so much time deciding what to buy whenever I went shopping. It was a stressful and infuriating experience sometimes.

The same would happen whenever I had to buy gifts. I felt pressured to spend certain amounts based on what other people had spent on me, even if it was more than I could afford. It made me feel guilty about how much I was spending and ashamed of how much I could afford to spend. Buying a gift for someone can be a bit of a minefield.

It's easy to overthink things. Are you spending enough on them? What if they spend more on you? Does it make me look like I don't care enough? We put way too much emphasis on the money part rather than the thought, the effort, or the gesture itself. So even when I would find the perfect gift, I'd feel guilty if it was under budget and buy something else for the sake of my financial guilt. I felt compelled to spend the exact same amount on each person to avoid anyone feeling unloved or hard done by.

Nowadays, I focus more on what I'm buying rather than how much I'm spending. If it is something they really want, that's more important than how much I've spent. I reason with myself that there is no point in buying something they don't need or particularly want for the sake of it. I'm conscious of not over-contributing to waste culture (I'm trying to be more environmentally conscious). By removing the financial guilt, I can enjoy the act of gift-giving much more without feeling so anxious or stressed. After all, it is meant to feel good to give someone a gift. I've always felt that spending time with someone is way more valuable than any gift you give them.

I was fortunate with my closest friends because we don't really buy each other gifts. Maybe it's a guy thing or a British thing, but we don't worry about that. Our birthdays are all about getting together and enjoying each other's company. We might buy the odd birthday card or an alcoholic drink, but there is no expectation or pressure. It's always about enjoying our time together. I think removing that expectation makes it much more appreciated when we do receive a gift, and it feels much more special when we buy one and we get to see their genuine reaction to it.

I experienced a bit of a culture shock when I started to get closer to my European friends. I was added to a WhatsApp group asking everyone to contribute towards a gift for someone. I was a little taken aback because although I loved the idea of it, I didn't like the peer pressure. I didn't feel that close to this person to buy them a gift, and I already felt anxious about money. My only options were to contribute and feel uncomfortably pressured into doing so, or risk upsetting or offending them by not. It should have been an innocent and nice gesture, but I felt anxious about spending money I hadn't planned to spend. Then I felt guilty for feeling that way. It felt silly, and I was ashamed of the whole situation.

But the most awkward moment was when one of my good Spanish friends was getting married. This threw me into an unexpected culture clash. I was so happy to be invited and was excited by the prospect of attending a wedding abroad with different traditions to my own culture. But when I was told that I was expected to provide a wedding gift worth around €120 to €150, I almost had a heart attack.

I was shocked because in British culture there are little to no expectations on the value of a gift; typically you are asked to give what you can or you feel comfortable with. We all know that getting married is an expensive affair, but so is attending the event when you consider the cost of your outfit, travel, accommodation, the evening bar, and the gift. Not to mention the obligatory stag or hen do abroad and the possibility of multiple weddings to attend.

We appreciate the effort it takes for people to be there. Whereas in many European countries, it is expected that the wedding party contribute a sizeable amount to effectively cover the cost of the whole wedding. It is a nice gesture, but if you're attending more than one it can be quite costly, especially if it is abroad. I understand the concept though, because if all the same guests attend each other's weddings, it probably works itself out in a way, but it wasn't something I was used to.

I suddenly found myself in an awkward situation. I felt uncomfortable and uneasy paying that amount, but I also felt obliged to do so. I didn't want to offend my friends, and I didn't want to damage our relationship. The whole thing made me feel really anxious. But they were close friends, so I realised the best thing I could do was to speak to them about it.

I explained how it worked in my culture and how uncomfortable I felt with it, and I also listened to their point of view on it. In the end, we agreed to a compromise. I contributed more than I would normally, and they accepted a little less in return. We understood how each other felt and our friendship never suffered because of it. So now, I am a lot more comfortable being upfront about these things; being open and honest with my friends rather than letting things build up inside.

Had I not had this conversation, I may have paid it but resented them for pressuring me into it or offended them and damaged our friendship. Instead, I did what was right for our friendship and what was right for my mental health. We need to learn to be more supportive and understanding of each other when it comes to money.

When you're a kid, you don't understand where money comes from or how hard is to get it. So when you see your friends with all the latest technology, you get jealous and upset about it. As a parent, you can feel pressured into providing for your children. You can easily feel bad about not giving them what they want and compare yourself to other parents. But we shouldn't feel guilty or embarrassed. My parents taught me the importance of money, and I learnt to accept that we may not get a brand-new PlayStation when our friends did, but there'd be a good chance we'd get it the following Christmas. If anything, it taught me patience, humility, and appreciation for what they did for us.

As an adult, it is easy to feel bad about wasting money. I used to feel guilty that I'd wasted so much money on buying DVDs for escapism when I was depressed. There were many purchases like that. I used to look back on them, thinking that if only I hadn't wasted that money, I could have bought something else that really matters. I've learnt to let go of things like that. In the case of the DVDs, I see it as needed escapism and a learning experience, but I no longer hold it against myself. That is stress I don't need; it's only holding me down.

For a long time I wasn't earning as much as I thought I should be, so I was always cautious with my spending. This meant that spending money on myself became a bit of a battle, and I would often talk myself out of purchases. I would deprive myself of little joys because I couldn't justify the expenditure. But occasionally it helps to spend a little on yourself as a treat or a reward for all the hard work you do. I still ask myself if something is worth the money; if I'm genuinely going to get positive use out of it. But I also remind myself of something a friend said to me once. She talked about enjoying your own money and allowing yourself to have things that you really want because it's your money; you've earned it and you can choose how to spend it. So, I put less pressure on myself now when it comes to money, and it feels good not to worry about it so much. I've removed a lot of the stigma and the guilt surrounding money, and I've learnt to be less critical of myself. I've learnt to trust myself with my own money.

Lessons Learned

- Try not to compare your income or finances to others. Appreciate what you have and not what you don't.

- Lower your financial expectations, both for how much you earn and how much you think you need to spend.

- When buying gifts, focus on the meaning and purpose of the gift and not on how much you've spent on it. Don't pressure yourself into overspending.

- Talk through financial conflicts with friends and family, and try to see things from each other's perspectives. Consider each other's culture and find a common ground.

- It's ok to treat yourself from time to time and enjoy the money you've worked hard to earn.

- Trust yourself with money, and don't overthink it.

True Friendship

As you get older, the old wisdom you heard when you were young but understandably ignored starts to resonate more and more. "You can count your real friends on one hand." I remember hearing this on numerous occasions, which I subsequently laughed off with sheer confidence and denial. When you are young, the thought of having such a small network of friends is alien, but as you get older, you begin to understand the truth behind it.

When you are young, your social life tends to be at its most active, and you are constantly meeting new people through education, work, hobbies, and social engagements. But as people start to get older, their priorities shift from social fun to stability and comfort. Relationships begin to blossom, careers progress, and individual free time starts to shrink. As relationships begin to grow and become more committed, they also become the focal point of individual lives and progress towards marriage and family life. So, keeping in touch and remaining a relevant and core part of your friends' everyday life becomes much more difficult.

Your lives begin to grow apart, and staying in touch becomes more of an effort, which is when friendships begin to fade.

People get caught up in their own lives, and keeping up regular communication with friends who you rarely see in person becomes less of a conscious priority as time passes. One week easily becomes a month, and then a year. As time goes by without any form of interaction, we start to question the relationship and our right to reconnect. Has it been too long? Do they still want to hear from me? They haven't contacted me, is it worth it? We talk ourselves out of it as though communication has an expiry date.

Social media has however helped to change the landscape a little, allowing you to remain connected at a distance. You are able to see snippets of your friends' lives and retain that feeling of their presence in your own life. The worldwide social lockdowns of the 2020/21 pandemic emphasised the strength and importance of these modern forms of communication. Video calls, online gaming, and social media allow us to remain connected no matter the distance, and with very little effort we can still be a part of each other's lives. But it still requires some effort. Someone has to instigate it; be willing to reach out and say, "Let's chat; let's catch up."

Ego can play an underlying role in the end of a friendship because sometimes, someone will convince themselves that the other person should make the effort. We feel that they should want to be a part of our lives, and we can resent the idea of having to be the one who puts themselves out there to initiate contact every time.

For a long time, I resented the fact that people relied on me to organise get-togethers. I felt that people took it for granted, and in a way, they took me for granted. They would tell me that I love organising things, but that wasn't the case, I was just the only one actively willing to make the effort. This was because I was worried that if I did not do it, nobody would, and as the only single one of the group who has struggled with loneliness and depression, I dreaded the thought of missing out. I feared what my life would become without my friends being an active part of it.

I didn't enjoy organising, but I was good at it, and I at least enjoyed the thought of adventure and planning these fun occasions would give me something to look forward to. But for a while, I began to take offence to it. I resented the onus my friends would automatically put on me, expecting me to always be the one to carry the burden and the stress of organising these events. Even though everyone benefited from them, I would rarely get the thank you I needed to soothe my resistance to the role of the organiser.

I began to reason that they didn't care as much as I did; that they were more comfortable with the thought of living their life without me than I was without them. I believed that I valued our friendship more than they did. I would go on hiatus to see if someone would step up, but often it would lead to barren periods of me wishing I'd sucked up my feelings and made the effort as usual. But I also felt deeply hurt and concerned that they did not return the love; that I would eventually lose them and be alone.

I read somewhere that being the person who your friends rely on to bring everyone together doesn't have to be a negative thing. It is not necessarily because they don't want to make the effort; it might just not be in their nature as much as it is in yours. People can get wrapped up in their own little worlds with all the everyday stresses and worries that can occur, so their social lives drop to the back burner.

So, I decided that it was ok to accept my role as the organiser within my friendship group, because the outcome is a positive one. I bring us all together so we can remain an important presence in each other's lives and continue to make memories together. Further to this, I spoke with my friends and I told them how I felt. I told them that I felt like I was being taken for granted and that I needed to see them make some effort too. This helped, because not only did my friends now understand how I felt, but I was more comfortable with taking on the ownership of organising things. I no longer resented it, which removed the negative feelings and the self-reflecting worry that would usually follow. And as I embraced my role, I began to enjoy the freedom of control. I became more selective with when, whom, or what we would do. Instead of trying to please everyone all the time, I could choose activities that fitted in with individual availability and personal interests.

During some of my darker periods in my 20s, I became more adept at maximising my social life by utilising my different friendship groups to ensure I had at least one or two social gatherings each week. This is because, during those times that I was feeling low or depressed, I knew that I needed my friends around me. I needed someone to talk to. I needed the occasional distraction or the release of negative energy. I needed that source of comfort and positivity in my life. So, I put in a lot of additional effort to keep my communication open with all my friends. I organised get-togethers days, weeks, or months in advance. I wanted to enjoy life, but I also knew that if I didn't make the effort and the invites didn't come often enough, I would be left alone feeling sorry for myself. I would be more vulnerable to the negativity taking over. Instead, I needed to be active; I needed to put in the work to improve my life. I learnt to understand and value the importance of my social life to my mental health.

As you get older and your friendships begin to change or fade away, you become more aware of the people you miss the most; the ones who really matter and who enrich your life. Your friendship circle shrinks, and you start to identify the people who mean the most to you. Conversely, you also start to identify the friendships that are fickle or even damaging.

As you mature and experience kicks in, identifying those more toxic relationships becomes much easier and more intuitive. You have less patience for negative people and fewer reservations about cutting them out of your life. Your tolerance for these people becomes limited, and rightly so. It is very important for your mental health to surround yourself with positive people and to remove those negative and toxic influences from your life.

The best friendships are with those who will be there for you when you truly need them; the ones who will forgive your shortcomings and support you in trying times. People who will check in on you; who will actually make an effort and show you that they care. Friendships should be 50/50. You should both contribute to it and benefit from it equally. As your friendship circle begins to shrink, there is no need to panic, because those that remain are the most meaningful and powerful relationships. You can always continue to meet new people and make new friends; just don't change yourself to fit in with others. Find people who add positivity to your life.

I've also learnt to give these guys a break. For a long time during my depression, I felt anger and frustration towards my friends. They would always say the wrong thing, and they would never give me what I was looking for. Now I know better. I can't expect everyone to understand or relate to my specific mental health challenges. How can I expect them to know the right words to say or how to act when I'm feeling down? How can I expect them to know when I'm struggling if I myself was unable to identify it for so long? I've learnt not to hide it, not to be ashamed of my struggles, and to trust my friends and be more open with them, but I've also learnt not to expect solutions from them. They are all doing their best to understand and are making a conscious effort to show support. I'm able to appreciate that, and I try to consider the role of each friendship.

Like I did with myself, I know which of my friends are more adept at listening, which friends are the best placed to offer some escape or distraction, and which ones are a source of positivity and inspiration. So, I can't expect someone who hasn't experienced anything like what I've struggled with to know what to say or how to help me. That isn't their fault, and I won't judge them for it. I do have friends who truly understand; who have experienced their own battles, and I have other sources and outlets to help me deal with that side of myself. I embrace the uniqueness of each friendship, and I know who to speak to about different matters, but I'm always open and honest with each of them.

As we learn to talk about our mental health and become more comfortable with being vulnerable with the ones we love, we also need to accept that everyone is still learning. Not everyone will be able to relate or understand. We have different strengths, and that's ok.

Whilst I have accepted my role as the organiser and I have learnt to open up about my mental health, I have also identified communication as one of my biggest strengths, whereas listening is one of my areas for improvement. I am a strong communicator, but I'm not always good at listening. The conversations I'm best at are the ones I can contribute to confidently or passionately. This is because I'm also a natural problem solver. I'm always looking for the solution and trying to help, but my experiences with mental health have taught me that sometimes we just need someone to listen. Even though my heart is in the right place and I want to help, sometimes all I need to do is listen and show my support as a friend.

This is something I've become more aware of as I've been able to reflect on my own experiences. It is an area for improvement that I have identified for myself, and because I am aware of it, I can make more of a conscious effort to work on it. My battle with depression has at times given me this false ego, convincing myself that because I have been through my own battles it somehow permits my urge to problem-solve. But having spoken to other people about their issues, I have remained aware of my efforts to listen more closely. I remind myself that just because I have been through something similar, it does not mean that I can solve their problems for them; I still need to listen.

Everyone's experience is different, and as much as I want to make their pain go away, it is not my responsibility, and I should not punish myself if I am unable to help. If

I have helpful advice and they want to hear it, I'm happy to share it. I will always show them my support, be there for them, and encourage them to keep going. After all, I know how much power there is in just talking about it. I understand the strength it takes to do so, so I will keep listening.

The global pandemic and the introduction of social distancing encouraged me to address another issue. I was always reluctant to speak on the phone. I was never comfortable with it. I hated talking on the phone or seeing myself on video; I would always try to avoid it, preferring WhatsApp and emails over phone calls. But the pandemic quarantine forced me to address that issue. As its value became more apparent and its popularity increased, I soon began to embrace it. As we all felt the strain of being forced to isolate ourselves away from other human beings, the value of speaking to someone on the phone or to see their face over a video call increased immensely.

I took it upon myself to encourage my friends and family to connect over video calls, not just for my benefit but for theirs too, and it was the closest I'd felt to many of them for a while. I overcame my fear of speaking on the phone, and I threw aside my reluctance to be the instigator. I brought us all closer together.

Thankfully since then, people have become more open to communicating remotely. It should no longer remain an excuse; we are lucky to have the technology to connect us with people from all over the world. I think we can all now see the value in connecting with a loved one, whether it is a five-minute chat or an entire quiz night with friends, it can make a big difference to your mindset. It is obviously not a replacement for seeing people in person; we should always make the effort to see each other because it strengthens our bond. But when it isn't possible, making the effort to have a video call can go a long way to reaffirm that bond and remind ourselves of the value of those friendships and the love that already exists in our life.

Finally, as a single man in my early 30s, I have learnt that keeping an active social life is more difficult now. To begin with, as my friends began to get married and have kids; as they moved further away to different cities or countries, I found myself momentarily lost. The people who I was closest to were now physically further away, and making new friends in my 30s felt like a difficult task. Meeting people of a similar age with similar interests was more challenging.

Now that I am a little older and more mature, I want different things from friendship and my social life. Finding people to fit into my life seamlessly is difficult, but not impossible. I still have plenty of freedom, and finding other people with a similar degree of flexibility as well as sharing interests are hard to come by.

It took me some time to let go of the social dynamic of my 20s and to embrace the new construct of the 30s. I have accepted that spontaneous adventures with my closest friends will be a rare phenomenon from now on. I've let go of the old version of our friendships and accepted the newer, evolved version. Because ultimately, my friends are happy. They have found love and settled down, and I could never resent them for that. I'm happy that they are happy.

My expectations have changed, and although I may encourage my friends to join me on adventures, I no longer feel rejected or hurt if they decline my offers. I am more flexible with them and also with myself. I understand that their priorities have changed, but I know that we are still friends and they still care about me. Having spent time with my married friends and with my niece and nephew also, I know how much time and energy is required. I am able to put myself in their shoes and give them more leeway.

Lessons Learned

- As you get older, friendships can drift apart as our lives progress, but don't hold that against your friends.

- The best friendships are worth holding on to. Make the effort to keep in touch, and keep them an active part of your life.

- No matter how long it has been, if you want to reach out to a friend or to reignite an old friendship, go for it.

- Accept your role within the group and be understanding of your friends' situations.

- Give your friends a break and let go of old social expectations. Try to evolve with your friends as their lives begin to change.

- Communicate with your friends about how you feel. They won't know you're struggling unless you tell them.

- Let go of your assumptions and be there for your friends. Listen and show them you care.

- Embrace modern technology and stay connected, but always make the extra effort to see each other in person.

- Take responsibility for your share of the friendship, and don't be afraid to work on yourself.

The Right Help

By now you know that when I first started to struggle with depression, I was only a teenager; about 17 years old. Whilst I was already trying to deal with the usual challenges that come with being a teenager, I was also faced with new feelings and emotions that I hadn't heard much about, let alone experienced before. Even as a young adult in my 20s, I struggled to learn how to deal with everything I was going through, and it took me a long time to understand what it was that I was feeling. It is even harder to then be able to admit that you are struggling. Whether a teenager, a man, or an independent adult, it can be a very hard thing to.

These days, there is a lot more information out there that can help you to understand what mental health looks like and how you can treat it. And many more people are aware and more understanding of it, so it should be a little easier than it used to be to talk about it with your friends and your family. I would definitely encourage people to do that. But I can still understand how it might be a difficult, intimidating, or an uncomfortable experience for some. But even if you do start to talk more openly about it with your loved ones, it is still worth considering whether you are getting the right help that you need.

Sometimes, our friends or families can find it hard to relate or even comprehend what we are feeling. Often their attitude or behaviour towards it is clouded by their desire to want the best for you and their urge to fix it. And to be fair to them, it is hard to know what to say. It can be difficult to see a loved one struggle, but we should still seek out these conversations so we can all be comfortable with it and we can learn together. But if you feel that the support and comfort you are getting is not enough; if it is not helping you to improve, then seeking the right help is the next step.

Reading a book written by someone who has dealt with many of their own struggles can help. So can researching the subject and reading professional sources online, such as your local health service or specialist charity websites. But better yet is to find someone with whom you can speak openly and honestly about the subject; likely someone who has experienced similar things. They may not be able to give you the perfect advice, but they can relate better, and sometimes, just speaking to someone who has been through something similar can make a huge difference. That person could be a friend or it could be a community support group.

Speaking to a professional should also be a consideration. These days there is very little stigma surrounding therapy. Many European cultures already embrace it as a normal thing to do (like going to the gym for your brain). Many fully functioning successful people swear by it; even the English football team has a therapist. In fact, therapy is becoming more and more common for elite athletes and high-stress professions. It can be expensive, but when it comes to your health, it may very well be worth it. As adults, we have a lot of stress in our lives. We have many responsibilities to juggle and a lot of thoughts and feelings to contend with every day. Therapy gives us an outlet for much of that.

We have all embraced the importance of seeking help when it comes to our physical health. Whether that be a doctor, a physiotherapist, a personal trainer, or a sports coach; it is widely accepted. That's because we understand the benefit of gaining external, professional insight and support. We need to treat our mental health in the same way. It is ok to ask for help, because the healthier your mind is, the happier your life will be.

Lessons Learned

- Your mental health is just as important as your physical health, and it requires regular upkeep.

- Continue to read about it to educate yourself. Read and listen to expert advice services online.

- Use mental health charity resources. Speak to a helpline; they have people who are trained to talk about mental health.

- Speak with other people who have experienced similar things.

- Join mental health community support groups.

- Trust your friends and talk to them about how you feel and what you are struggling with.

- Consider therapy; many people swear by it. It can be a valuable outlet.

- Speak to a doctor if you're concerned about how you're feeling.

- Look out for yourself and your mental health. Don't ignore it; take action.

Self-Awareness

I consider self-awareness to be one of the most defining traits of intelligence and a crucial ingredient to genuine maturity; being able to identify your impact on others, seeing beyond your subjective point of view, and understanding how others may perceive you. But further to this is understanding how someone else may think or feel even if those thoughts and feelings are alien to you; putting yourself in someone else's shoes whilst knowing and being honest with yourself are truly important for your own happiness and progression through life. Accepting your flaws and taking pride in your strengths is also a part of self-awareness and self-love.

A small task that I set myself turned out to be very eye-opening, and it changed my perspective of myself. It is something that I would encourage everyone to try. All you need to do is to make a list of everything you like about yourself. I feel we always focus on the negatives. We regularly criticise ourselves or compare ourselves to others in a negative light, and we rarely build ourselves up. Why not try and focus on the positives? I guarantee you will be surprised at just how many positives you can find. You may just uncover your real love for yourself. Think about your personality, your attitude and behaviour in different scenarios, your relationships, your accomplishments, your physical attributes; all the things you like about yourself.

Force yourself to write down at least 10 things you like, and then think of a few more things and keep adding to them as you get older. Remind yourself of it regularly so when you do identify a negative, you can appreciate that you also have plenty of strengths. This will give you comfort and the power to work on your flaws. Try to see the positive side of things, including your flaws.

I have one or two possible negatives that I can see the positive side of, like my natural stubbornness. It can at times be a flaw, but it is one I am aware of, and so it is something I can influence and make a conscious effort to adjust when necessary. But it is also a positive because I refuse to give in easily. I am not easily influenced by others, and I have strength and resilience. I don't dismiss it as a negative that is a detriment to my personality; I appreciate its purpose and its role within me.

Being self-aware allows us to overcome our bad habits because we can identify them as behaviours or as characteristics that we need to work on. 'Crazy people don't know they are crazy', so they can't identify crazy behaviour. Learning to be self-aware is learning to understand who we are and to accept our place in the world.

This is something I am always working on because I have spent a large portion of my life worrying about myself, stressing over every little thing, and constantly battling with negativity. Often when I was doing well in my life, I still feared falling back into depression, and conversely, when

I was particularly happy or excited, I wanted to talk about it. My focus was still on me. Either I was trying to protect myself or I was trying to show people that I was doing well for a change. I would often focus too much on my own perspective in conversations or debates, which made me a little self-conscious.

So I began to look out for it more so that I could remind myself to listen more or to consider another person's perspective before sharing my own. It makes a huge difference to your emotional response if you can put yourself in someone else's shoes, especially during an argument; to be able to take a step back and say, ok I'm upset because of these reasons, but they are also upset because of these other reasons. Being able to consider why someone has said or done something in a certain way and to understand how certain events could have led them there can allow you to forgive a little more. It can help you to understand behaviours a little better, reminding you that we are all human and constantly affected by the individual worlds that we live in as well as the collective one we all share.

It helps to lighten the instinctive emotional response and minimises the offence we immediately feel. At least, this is what I have experienced. And challenging myself to see things from the point of view of others helps me to not only understand them better, but to share more rounded concepts and ideas; Thoughts that register beyond my selfish intentions.

It all comes from understanding yourself and being comfortable in your own skin. When you are readily able to admit your flaws and accept them openly, you are less exposed to the hurt of criticism; instead, you are more understanding of it. Being more comfortable with owning up to your mistakes and being able to appreciate someone else's perspective allows you to be a little more considerate and understanding.

It is something we all miss when we are struggling with our mental health. When you are depressed or struggling with issues that impact and inhibit your daily life, it can feel so frustratingly difficult to explain to other people what you are going through, and they are often unable to understand or relate in any way. Withholding judgement, listening with compassion, and providing a comfortable and supportive environment whilst being patient is the response we all need to feel comfortable opening up about our inner pain.

Lessons Learned

- Self-awareness is a sign of intelligence and maturity and is beneficial for your mental health.

- Seeing the big picture allows you to put yourself in the shoes of others and to process things better.

- Give yourself a moment to consider why someone has said or done what they have. Try to see things from their perspective.

- Write a list of everything you like about yourself and remind yourself of it regularly.

- Accept your strengths and your weaknesses as part of who you are.

- Identifying your flaws allows you the opportunity to work on them.

- Own up to your mistakes and take responsibility for your actions.

- Love yourself, but be mindful of your impact and influence on others.

Fight for Yourself

Don't forget to fight. Life is hard, especially if you are struggling with your mental health, but don't give up. Things can improve, and with every little improvement, you get that little bit stronger. It is a long fight, but one that gets better and easier the more you continue with it. There comes a point when we must realise that hoping, wishing, and dreaming isn't going to help. We know by now that the universe doesn't just hand us the life we want; we have to scrap, fight, and claw our way to the things we want. We just have to remind ourselves that we can do it, because there is so much worth fighting for. But we have to prepare ourselves and accept that the long journey ahead is going to be tough. It is going to test us, but we aren't going to let anyone or anything get in our way. We are on a mission to save ourselves from ourselves.

Let's not forget, there are many different things that we can do to work on ourselves and to strengthen our mental health and resilience. Accepting help from others is one of them, but there will be times when we may only be able to rely on ourselves. Some things can only be changed or achieved through our own efforts. These things won't miraculously happen, and time won't fix them, but good old fashioned hard work and determination will.

One of those times was when I was younger. I had been scrapping and fighting for years to rectify my career, to make up for my lack of a degree, and to get myself over the graduate-level barrier. I had worked hard and been patient and understanding, but enough was enough. I had done everything that had been asked of me, and I was no longer willing to wait.

I made my intentions clear to my line manager and to my team, and I asked for more responsibility and more opportunities. I wanted to continue to prove myself, and I wanted to build up enough undeniable evidence to support my case for my shot at a promotion. I persisted; I didn't shy away from a challenge. I asked for constructive feedback, accepted my areas for improvement, and I worked on them. I took all the advice I could get. I made it clear to everyone that I was going to do whatever was necessary to make this happen. And it paid off.

There were no more excuses and no possible reason to hold me back, and I finally got my shot. Before the interview, I made sure to maintain my performance levels. I asked for advice from those who had been through the process before, and I spoke with experienced interviewers. I memorised the job description and prepared my examples and answers for skills- and experienced-based questions. I left no stone unturned. I made sure that I was mentally prepared for the task at hand, and I gave myself the best possible chance of succeeding. And it worked.

I finally smashed the glass ceiling that had plagued my professional career for years. I would no longer be under the shadow of my university failure. It had been a huge mental barrier that I made for myself, but it was also a real issue that was holding back my progress. In the end, it was me who had to force the issue. I could no longer rely on my colleagues or my peers to get me there. I knew that it was down to me to prove myself and to give my employers no choice but to reward me for my efforts. Sometimes we just have to roll our sleeves up and put in our maximum effort.

It took me a long time to face one of the biggest barriers in my young life, but once I finally broke through it, a huge weight was lifted and I could see the light at the end of the tunnel. By resolving a core issue in one of the four pillars of my life, I was able to focus on the others. One thing at a time. No matter how little the change I made; it was progress. No matter how hard things would get, I knew that I could keep going. I did it before, and I'll do it again. I'll pick myself up, I'll dust myself off, and I'll go again and again and again because I won't let anything stop me. Because I'm worth it. And so are you. Keep going. Keep moving forward.

FIGHT FOR YOURSELF!

Lessons Learned

- It all starts with acceptance and every little change you make will make it that little bit easier.

- You have the power to change your life, no matter how hard it gets or how dark it may seem, there is always something you can do.

- Keep moving forward because no matter how hard it gets. It will take time, hard work and sacrifice, but it will be worth it.

- Remember the 4 Pillars, give your life structure and identify which areas need your attention.

- Put in the work and don't let anybody stop you. Be an unstoppable force of nature.

- Accept help from others.

- Remember that you do matter, you have value and you are worth fighting for!

The Things I've Learned

1. **Acceptance** really is the first and most important step to start the healing process.

2. The **Four Pillars**. Ensure that you always have at least one healthy centre in your life, whether it is at home, at work, in your love life, or in your social life. Focus your efforts on each area at a time and have patience. It takes time to build a happy life.

3. A healthy body fuels a healthy mind. What you eat and how much you exercise affects your mood and your mindset. It is your source of energy, and it is vital.

4. Communication really is key. Talking about your feelings with loved ones or with a professional will genuinely help you with the healing process.

5. Honesty is always the best philosophy. Being honest with yourself and the ones you care about most will build stronger foundations for long-lasting happiness.

6. Set yourself goals for the long and the short term. Give yourself something to aim for. Make a bucket list to ensure you are getting the most out of life.

7. Be realistic with your expectations. Don't put too much pressure on yourself and focus on the things you can control.

8. Be patient and persistent. It is going to take a lot of work and a lot of time to find your inner peace, but it is definitely worth fighting for.

9. Give yourself a break. Make sure your calendar is filled with things to look forward to, and make sure you take the time off when you need it and disconnect. Allow yourself to rest and recover.

10. 10. Immerse yourself in nature. Travel, have an adventure, and remind yourself of the beauty in the world.

11. Enjoy the little things. Celebrate every little success and use it to motivate you and keep you focused. And keep moving forward.

12. Surround yourself with good people. Remove the toxic and negative influences from your life.

13. Curate your social media. Only follow, watch, or engage with positive and inspirational people. Block,

remove, and avoid negative influences. Put yourself in control of this world.

14. Expand your world and change your perspective. Meet people from different backgrounds and different cultures, and learn from their experiences. See things from a different angle, and learn to see the bigger picture.

15. Make a list of everything positive about yourself; everything you like about yourself and your accomplishments. Remind yourself of the positives so you can find the strength to accept your flaws.

16. Never stop working on yourself. We are always growing and learning, and no one is perfect.

17. Forgive yourself for making mistakes and learn from the experience. Everybody makes mistakes; it is part of being human.

18. Embrace failure. If you want to succeed at anything, you must be willing to fail. Every failure is an important lesson, and it will help you to reach your goals.

19. Be in the moment. Let go of distractions and allow yourself to enjoy the moment while it is happening. You will miss it when it is gone.

20. Don't forget to listen. Avoid getting caught up in your own world too much, and listen to the ones you love;

show them that you are there for them too. Caring for others gives us strength and perspective.

21. Step out of your comfort zone more often. The only way you will find change is if you make it happen. Push yourself, get out of the safety of your own home, and put yourself out there.

22. Say yes more often. Do not let fear hold you back. Say yes to life and its opportunities, and be spontaneous from time to time.

23. Accept help. It is not your burden alone to carry and it is not weak to ask for help. We all rely on each other; we truly are stronger together.

24. Allow yourself to be vulnerable with your closest loved ones. Share the real you, talk about your insecurities, and be honest about your feelings. The strongest relationships are built on the strongest partnerships.

25. The past really is the past. Let go of the things you cannot change. Accepting them is the only way to move on. Value what you have gained since and move forward.

26. Only you have the power to change things. Do not wait for fate to intervene because it isn't going to. If something is not right in your life, it is up to you to work out how to change it.

27. Stop making excuses and get out of your own way. Do what you need to do to improve your life, even if it scares you.

28. It's ok to say no sometimes. Look out for yourself and don't let people take advantage of your generosity.

29. Be smart with your money and spend it on the things that really matter, but don't deprive yourself of life's little joys. Invest in the things that make you happy.

30. Learn to be more self-aware. Reflect on your thoughts, feelings, and behaviours, and understand your tendencies. Be aware of your impact on others and accept responsibility for your own actions.

31. Believe in yourself and your abilities. Accept compliments and listen to positive feedback. Acknowledge your efforts and enjoy the merits of your success.

Note that this list has 31 items. Even with my OCD tendencies I did not force an equal or round number because I've accepted that life isn't perfect and I can't change everything.

These are the most important lessons I have learnt over the last 16 or 17 years of my mental health journey. You may learn some of your own lessons; things that work well for you. This is not an exclusive or exhaustive list; it is just the knowledge that I have gained from my personal experience. They may not all work for you, but it should encourage you to know that there are so many possibilities out there for making changes and improving your life. No matter how difficult and how unlikely it may seem, there is hope. Don't give up. Believe in yourself and your loved ones and keep moving forward. Never stop fighting for yourself. You've got this!

Thank you for taking the time to read my book. I really hope you found it useful. I wish you all the best with your mental health journey.

Please consider showing your support by leaving an honest review where you purchased the book from or on your favourite store. Please also consider telling your friends about it and sharing it on social media.

Sincerely,
Simon George

Acknowledgements

First, I would like to acknowledge myself and all the hard work I've put in over the years. I have been through a lot and struggled for large parts of my adult life, and yet no matter how hard it has gotten; no matter how low or defeated I felt, I have never given up. I have come out of it all a much stronger, healthier, and happier man than I would have ever been having not had my struggles. My mental health is in a good place, but I will never stop working on it, and I am proud of myself for what I have achieved.

I am so proud to have written this book. It was probably one of the biggest items on my bucket list, and when I first dreamt about it, I didn't really believe it was realistic or possible. It has taken a lot of hard work and a lot of time and patience, but I have stuck with it and persisted, and I am so happy that I did because it is an amazing accomplishment. It was challenging at times but also rewarding, and I have learnt a lot from the experience.

Second and probably most importantly, I would like to thank you, the reader. I want to thank you for entrusting me with such an important subject. Whether you are trying to learn more about mental health for yourself or someone else or you are currently going through your own journey, thank you for choosing my book—I am truly honoured. I am not a celebrity, influencer, or a celebrated author, but I really hope you have found this helpful, and I wish you all the best with your journey. I encourage you to keep doing what you're doing. Never stop learning and never give up, because you're making great progress and heading in the right direction, even if at times it may not feel like it. Believe in yourself and trust in the process of healing.

I would also like to thank my editor, Susan. This is the first book I've ever written, and you've helped me to turn it into something I can be proud of. Your feedback and advice have not only given me confidence in the quality of my work, but you have also helped to take it to the next level. The look and feel of the book as well as the flow have all benefited from your valuable input, so thank you.

And finally, a big shout-out to my friend Mark. Thank you so much for taking the time to read the very first draft of this book. Thank you for the kind, supportive, and helpful feedback you gave me; it means a lot to me. Thank you for suggesting the idea of the chapter summaries—I think they turned out to be a great addition to the book. Cheers buddy.

I know the world is in a difficult place right now, and there are a lot of things we all collectively need to work on, but I encourage everyone to prioritise their mental health. Once we are all living in a healthier and happier mindset, we will be able to achieve so much more together.

Thank you once again and all the best.

Simon George